WRESTLING WITH WISDOM AT THE CROSSROADS

The Aphorisms and Poems of Malachi Montroy

CHILLY BILLY HOWELL

ROSE & PEARL
Publishing

Copyright © 2025 Chilly Billy Howell. All rights reserved.

No part of this publication may be reproduced, stored in a retrieval system, or transmitted in any form or by any means—electronic, mechanical, photocopy, recording, or otherwise—without prior written permission of the publisher, except in the case of brief quotations embodied in critical articles or reviews.

Hardcover ISBN: 978-1-969515-04-0

Cover art/design: Corinne Fikes

Cover photograph: Madge Marley Howell

Editing: Carolyn Wiley

Interior design/typesetting: Rose & Pearl Publishing

Publisher: Rose & Pearl Publishing, LLC • Senatobia, MS • roseandpearlpublishing.com

Permissions & inquiries: support@roseandpearl.net

First edition, November 2025

Printed in the United States of America

10 9 8 7 6 5 4 3 2 1

The views and opinions expressed in this book are those of the author and do not necessarily reflect the views of the publisher.

For Madge Marley Howell,

who believed in me when I was unbelievable.

Listen as Wisdom calls out!
Hear as understanding raises her voice!
On the hilltop along the road,
she takes her stand at the crossroads.

— PROVERBS 8:1-2

'Cause we're living in a world of fools breaking us down.

— BROTHERS GIBB

And it is not the voice of a priest or a prophet saying, 'These things are.' It is the voice of a dreamer and an idealist crying, 'Why cannot these things be?'

— G.K. CHESTERTON

CONTENTS

List of Poems   ix
Preparatory Note   xiii
Introduction   xv

DEVOTIONAL COMPANION   3

A GUIDELINE FOR APHORISMS   6

APHORISMS
Chapter 1   9
Chapter 2   16
Chapter 3   23
Chapter 4   29
Chapter 5   35
Chapter 6   41
Chapter 7   47
Chapter 8   53
Chapter 9   60
Chapter 10   66
Chapter 11   72
Chapter 12   79
Chapter 13   85
Chapter 14   92
Chapter 15   99
Chapter 16   106
Chapter 17   113
Chapter 18   120
Chapter 19   127
Chapter 20   134
Chapter 21   141
Chapter 22   148
Chapter 23   154
Chapter 24   161
Chapter 25   168
Chapter 26   175

Chapter 27	182
Chapter 28	189
Chapter 29	196
Chapter 30	203
Chapter 31	209
POEMS	219
Afterword	323
Acknowledgments	325
About the Author	327
Illustration Index	329

LIST OF POEMS

Soul of the Poet..219
The Elephant's Graveyard...221
Precarious the Sanity of He Who Walks Alone.........................222
Disease of More...223
Eye to Eye..225
Consumed by Him the Addict..227
At Our Creator's Beckon...229
Being Southern..230
God Showed Me Many Mountains...232
Things Done and Left Undone...234
Eternity Stranded in Time..235
Ode to a Fallen Kokopelli..236
Sin Whispers to Evil..237
If the World Goes Dark Tomorrow...238
I Yearn for the Heather Hills..240
Cemeteries at night...241
Peace Will Calm the Waters...242
My Dog Dandy...244
Rollercoaster Ride...245
What Threat Does a Hognose Pose..247
Who Is Rich Folks...248
I Saw Your Gaze Today...250

Only Guilty Man	251
Ides of May	252
Cowered by the Lying Tongue	254
I Thought I Had More Time	256
Tank Man	257
How Burned the Hands	259
Remorse	261
It Shouldn't Hurt	262
Where Is Annabelle	263
Victimization	264
Cellophane Blues	265
Casa De Macabre	266
Balancing Man and Earth	267
Look to the Heavens	268
Where Have All the Children Gone	269
Kayaking on Moon Lake	270
Salt Is Not the Devil	272
Mystery of Faith	273
House 'Tween the Hedges	274
Yolanda's Shriek	276
Drugs	278
Petulant Peter	278
I Hold the Foul Thing Dearer	280
She Called Me Daddy	281
Green Is All Around Me	282
The Things We Lose	284
Dandy and Daddy	285
Earl and Ginger, What a Pair	285
Never a Civil Word	286
I Lost Another Friend Today	287
The Soul of an Addict	289
My Heart a Seismic Seam	289
Hegemony Foul	290
Wide Awake on Prednisone	291
A Pleasant Wilderness	292
Sitting on the Square	294
The Cabal of Vile	296
Acid Rain, Mammon's Stain	297

Blood, Blood, and More Blood...298
The Luddites Have It Right..303
To the Unknown Waitress...304
I Pose for Others...306
Winter Arrives...307
Hand-stitched Lacerations...308
Anthem of First-World Shame...309
Covid-19 Belly Blues...311
Hairline Fractures..312
Hate Has No Color...314
Feet Marching High on Poplars...315
The Days of Wine and Roses Nevermore...............................316
My Sister is Submissive...317
Grumbling and Complaining...318
Shades Are What We Recognize..319
Alipius Knew Better..320
Seen and Unseen...321

PREPARATORY NOTE

There is nothing new under the sun.

— SOLOMON

The Aphorisms and Poems of Malachi Montroy can loosely be regarded as unplanned, philosophical, random thoughts penned over about a 10-year period. If any seem to resemble quotes penned by others, it is merely coincidental; all were original to me when I thought them.

I profess no profundity in most of them, admit many are pedantic, and there was never any intention of doing anything with the thoughts, poems, and aphorisms other than to record them, as I thought and felt them. They were random reflections, jotted down on a smartphone, chronicling capricious thoughts, responding to my life as I lived it.

A while back, my wife and I were awakened to the possibility of "doing something" with them. We were reading the Proverb chapter of the day corresponding with the day of the month, when Chapter 8 was illuminated.

It referred to Wisdom taking her stand at the Crossroads. Where we live in the Mississippi Delta is referenced worldwide as the epicenter of the Faustian myth of the Crossroads. A paradox is evident in our being known for a devilish myth and for being in the center of the Bible Belt, where Faith is a commonality among the races, genders and age groups.

PREPARATORY NOTE

According to the Bible, Wisdom was the first thing created by the Godhead and was referred to as a she. The Bible, along with a plethora of classical works, consistently refers to wisdom as "the thing" to get to live an ordered, successful, peaceful, virtuous life. And Jesus, who is God, is referred to as Wisdom.

Why Wisdom at the Crossroads? Crossroads represent directional choices, often made at critical life junctures, where we must decide which way to go—farther and further down the actual and metaphorical road.

Malachi has wrestled, still wrestles, and hopes to keep wrestling with Wisdom at the Crossroads and anywhere paths intersect, and decisions must be made. When we wrestle with decisions regarding the particulars and the universals in daily living, we contend with many of the elements seen in the several conflicts of literature. The most significant conflicts implied in the why of this book are: Character vs. Self, Character vs. Fate, and Character vs. Supernatural (my will versus God's will).

In my wrestling, I am better prepared to make decisions about the paths to take in pursuit of Truth, beauty and right living. This was the unrecognized catalyst for keeping the raw content of this book for over ten years.

INTRODUCTION

"Wrestling with Wisdom at the Crossroads" has nothing, yet everything, to do with the Faustian Myth, the fabled Crossroads, where Wisdom and decision wrestle with Determinism, where Wisdom grapples with sophistry, where Truth tussles with specious philosophy, and black and white contend with perceivable shades of pragmatic gray!

Just as the Biblical Patriarch, Jacob, wrestled with a corporeal manifestation of God for an entire night until he received God's blessing, so we, who desire to have it, must wrestle with what biology, environment and God have likely determined for us. This book strives to reflect my engagement with free will to choose the best path laid before me, as I have grappled with God's Wisdom proffered—past, present and future.

I believe God has given mankind enough free will to choose many of the paths life presents. As a Sovereign, He knows the outcome; yet, He gives us options to take paths in line with and often antithetical to His will. He does not desire automatons to serve Him, but wants His most marvelous creation, created in His image, to intentionally choose to search for, ask for, wrestle and groan for His best for us on life's short ride.

One could consider these aphorisms, arranged chronologically, as random discussion starters in intimate group settings, or as a catalyst for individual or corporate reflection. The original poems, augmented by the artwork and illustrations by my wife Madge, are not necessarily understood, and that's okay; they

INTRODUCTION

were never planned, rushed forth at unexpected moments, and in hindsight, appear more spiritual in nature than my other musings.

I am seven years sober and drug free, so the narrative embedded in over 2,700 aphorisms and 77 poems reflects the before and after; however, the before Recovery from substance abuse still reflects my long-held, Judeo-Christian world view, even when I poorly have lived it.

Think of this book as a rolling narrative, like the confluence of many rivers, where each particular aphorism stands alone, yet contributes as an important drop to the universal stream of one man's paddle through life's eddies, whirlpools, thunderstorms, redemptive rains, still waters, and always choices to be made and unknowns to contend; yet, with consistent metaphysical access to Wisdom and direction…

The Devotional Companion can be used in settings where one or two or possibly more are gathered. It provides a loose framework about how to engage with others through shared devotions, readings, discussions, etc. relative to wrestling with Wisdom.

This is my story…well, kind of…

DEVOTIONAL COMPANION

A helpful resource designed to guide one or more people—including families—as they discuss, reflect on, and apply Scripture and other readings to their daily lives.

The intent of this devotional companion is to be a tool for those who want to grow in their Faith or are exploring whether the beginning of a faith journey is right for them.

BACKGROUND

My wife and I began a daily devotional first thing in the morning soon after COVID hit, and churches began closing doors and requiring "distancing." This led us to begin our day with prayer, scripture reading, and discussion about what we read. Truly, for both of us, this is the highlight of our day: a silver lining that began during a period of societal unfamiliarity and confusion.

May the reader see what Madge and I do as a prompt for how one may go about drawing closer to God. We presume to tell no one how they should "live, move, and have their being." This is just what works for us and continues to help these two pilgrims on our journey to Eternity.

HOW WE DO IT

NOTE: While we discuss our readings for the day, we did not always. The most important thing is to read; then, if comfortable, feel free to discuss the readings.

1. Light a candle

We light a candle, get our day's devotional resources at hand, and place our phones to the side.

2. Pray

We begin with prayer. I usually do the initial praying out loud. Beginning with thanks, then a fairly standard (though not scripted) daily set of prayers for loved ones, those needing healing, supplication for local, state, national and worldwide leaders to govern wisely, prayers for our day, all followed by a prayer that God would open His Word (the Bible) to us, culminating with the Lord's

Prayer (From the Gospel of Matthew in the New Testament, a prayer that Jesus Christ told his followers to pray):

"Our Father which art in heaven, Hallowed be thy name. Thy kingdom come. Thy will be done in earth, as it is in heaven. Give us this day our daily bread. And forgive us our debts, as we forgive our debtors. And lead us not into temptation, but deliver us from evil: For thine is the kingdom, and the power, and the glory, for ever. Amen."

NOTE: We have learned through this daily devotional that we hear and understand more clearly when we listen interactively with others. We suggest that reading out loud helps with the cognitive process.

3. Read from Psalms

We read a verse or an entire chapter from the book of Psalms in the Old Testament. We briefly discuss what we think the psalmist intended, how it improves our understanding of God's eternal nature, and how we can apply it to our individual and corporate lives.

4. Read from the Proverb of the day

Read a verse or two, or the whole chapter, from Proverbs in the Old Testament matching the day of the month—for example, Proverbs 1 on the 1st, Proverbs 2 on the 2nd, and so forth. We discuss the inherent wisdom in the reading of the day, sometimes in depth and sometimes just an acknowledgment.

5. Read from the New Testament

Read a selection from the New Testament. In the past, we began with the four Gospels, then worked our way through to the end of The Revelation of John. Now, we go book by book, with no set reading length, just to a point of discussion.

6. Read from Christian apologetic literature for insight

Our devotional ends with a passage from the literature we are reading and discussing together, like G.K. Chesterton's *Orthodoxy,* C.S. Lewis's *Mere Chris-*

tianity, Francis Schaeffer's *How Should We Then Live?*, or an essay from the online journal, The Imaginative Conservative: "For those who seek the Truth, the Good and the Beautiful." To further spark discussion, we reflect on one or two Malachi aphorisms chosen from the 31 chapters that match the day of the month.

We limit our portions to the time constraints of the day and to the depth of what we just read. Sometimes the complexities inherent in the reading require more distillation to clarify its essence.

THAT IS PRETTY MUCH IT! The important thing is not a set formula, but the intent to pray, read, discuss and connect around God's word and other seminal writings.

A GUIDELINE FOR APHORISMS

A Guideline for using the Aphorisms

Select one of Malachi Montroy's aphorisms within the chapter which corresponds with the current day of the month.

Read. Reflect. Discover.

APHORISMS

Aphorism: A concise and often witty statement
of wisdom or opinion embodying
a general truth or astute observation.

Chapter 1

1. Sad begets sad.

2. I'm the sorriest man I know; I just don't let everybody agree with me.

3. I am thrilled a day will come when I won't be depressed about being depressed; I am depressed knowing I have so much to be thankful for.

4. The only thing you can trust is the Truth and sometimes in stretching it one can best tell it.

5. There's a battle every day in my head.

6. Hey man, I'm depressed as hell, but at least I've started back drinking; surely that will help.

7. Flirting with darkness is like kissing the cold lips of the dead.

8. If going to church regularly doesn't help one treat others and their property with respect, then something is not working.

9. There is a big difference between understanding something and condoning it.

10. I am an extremist who loathes extremes.

11. The nuances of Creation are all the more exotic because of Design.

12. The less I hide what is already apparent, the more I may see what I am attempting to hide.

13. The best thing is to raise kids right, and then love them fiercely when they do wrong.

14 Some things remain unsaid this side of Heaven.

15 Mississippi Delta: Where if the booze doesn't get you, the sugar will.

16 I'm just one pitiful voice about to squeak in the wilderness.

17 It's not that I prefer my own company; it's just easier than being around people.

18 Shining my own butt is hard work. It's always a risk.

19 Hey man, I died a long time ago.

20 My wife is my life.

21 In a world where country music matters, he's top-water bait.

22 Nobody messes with my head more than I do.

23 If they won't listen to Ben Carson, then they sure won't listen to me.

24 The more depressed I become, the more depressed I become, as I remember that God is sufficient to deal with my depression; yet, I remain depressed, because I am depressed while being blessed more than most folks.

25 Depression for the believer is a double-edged sword; cognitively knowing we are depressed when we shouldn't be engenders a deeper depression.

26 Self-pity is devil's bait for the depressed believer.

27 Lord, please teach me what to do with "sad," while living among so much plenty.

28 Hey man, I'm not sad or depressed; I'm sitting in the dark drinking bourbon by myself and listening to "Simple Man." What could possibly be wrong!

29 Being depressed sure eats up a lot of my time.

30 It's much easier to tell a lie than a tale, even when the tale includes plenty of the former.

31 To understand thyself is to understand others; to understand others is to understand one's self.

32 I only see Grace in the rearview mirror, except for the occasional faces floating in the backseat full of recriminations and haunting.

33 For a sensitive child, heartbreak is a given regardless of upbringing; I remain broken.

34 Look to the past for strength in the future.

35 My brain is part sponge and part Teflon.

36 Some lifestyles make as much sense to me in the natural as a gorilla French kissing a chicken. But I say let folks be free to be who they want to be. This is America.

37 Scripture tells me, "Why not rather be wronged." Whew…

38 I may feel like a piece of crap, but I am not one. God loves me; this I know.

39 The silence of family and friends for even meager accomplishments speaks volumes.

40 Only takers and the ignorant desire Socialism.

41 I am not creative or artistic; I just check stuff out sometimes.

42 I bet cows don't get tired at the end of the day from thinking.

43 Just the often memory of the broken, pinkish, Prelapsarian Princess shoe of my youngest, estranged daughter, where light is diffused due to the excrement of broken relationships—but for God, I would check out of here... It's often more than I can handle.

44 Memories, good or bad, are a distant Dad's dark place.

45 I wish I could get inside the mind of someone else to help me better understand my own.

46 My mind is the struggle.

47 Only God can bring redemption out of horror.

48 I'm sorry I squandered my life; I might have been a good preacher—a pastor, not so much.

49 Stones get heavier when they also represent the same sins peculiar to the thrower.

50 My scars quiver and flutter like cerise gills on a winter-dormant fish.

51 I seem to fear more for others when I am not myself mentally okay. Projection.

52 I'd better make peace with alienation, since I can't handle too much stimulation.

53 I am equal parts Eddie Haskell, Tom Sawyer, Huck Finn, Holden Caulfield, Pappy O'Daniel, and Eeyore.

54 I like trees, as they are so easy to be around.

55 I loathe my hypersensitivity.

56 My sanity is always in question; my lack of it is tempered only by God's goodness.

57 One problem I have in spades is that I want to know as much as possible with as little effort as possible with as much recognition as possible.

58 I can't judge the rest of my life by a couple of grey days in winter.

59 Whatever you ascribe to me may be true or untrue, but I am likely much worse than you imagine.

60 Prelapsarian belief in the goodness of man should have died with recognition of my own obsidian treasure trove of sins.

61 I am but a meretricious philosophical manqué who likely has never had an original thought. Specious, I am.

62 Only a "proud" young man would shoot a chipmunk with a 12-gauge shotgun.

63 I wouldn't sit around and listen to the devil if I knew it was he doing the talking; so I'm not going to sit around and listen to lying politicians or faux pundits who know they are lying with their forked tongues.

64 Come what may, I attest God has given me more days than I deserve or should have expected.

65 I am not tough enough to talk smack.

66 Just because some folks don't speak to me doesn't necessarily mean they're less than.

67 I need God more than most folks.

68 I don't have a problem with booze, because I drink all the time.

69 I may be bat-dung crazy, but they are too bat-dung crazy, and somebody has to draw the line. I am an artist.

70 It is not patronizing when you show almost obsequious respect to folks you love or respect, because you want them to really know you respect them—really know; because of preconceptions by those who don't know so much about such things, ignorance runs rampant.

71 I have a pugnacious exterior with a cowardly interior.

72 Sadly, I don't live in the present; I try to control the present.

73 Dude, it's about tares and wheat now.

74 People don't like when you share your own press. Heck, people don't like it when you simply get press.

75 I handle bad news worse than anybody I know.

76 A point of great internal angst for me is that so many of my egregious, self-centered behaviors and thoughts from my youth remain...

77 Even preachers gamble, and Achilles might have been a preacher, before he became a heel.

78 I love a job where I try to talk people out of buying my product—me.

79 Life explained, chronicled and shared is always just one person's thread, usually not the whole.

80 They appear stupid because they are heavily influenced by evil, which blinds them to Truth.

81 I wouldn't want to be a tare right now.

82 It's hard to reason with hard; once you become hard, you are hard, and hard has not got time for play.

83 Even my happiest thoughts contain volumes of sadness.

84 Not getting to raise my kids is like taking one's worst life moment and then saturating it in hot, bubbling acid.

85 I'm the most unlikely innkeeper; heck, I am the most unlikely anything.

Chapter 2

1. I reckon I am not really crazy; I am just not like anybody else.

2. "Down here" is about what's to come.

3. Sensitive kids get hard or die.

4. What befalls a sensitive boy can be as hard emotionally as times in '29.

5. There is little that will break you down and toughen you up more than "brothers" who crap on you.

6. Trying to get me to focus on a particular thought when I am holding court in my mind, which is galloping more quickly than a fast-moving kaleidoscope, is like trying to pinch the wind on a downhill rollercoaster.

7. It's okay for a conman to recognize another conman, but it is not okay to judge him with a crooked stick.

8. I con mostly for emotional safety, not so much for gain.

9. Spotting a conman is never hard for a conman.

10. I love an underdog, but I'll always pull for the top dog if he is the best, because he likely works hard to be the best.

11. Wind chimes may haunt, yet there is a distinct order to the sounds crafted by the unseen wind.

12. Making decisions when manic can lead to depression when depressed.

13 I am thankful not to be dependent on bureaucracies and the folks who "tend" them.

14 If I put myself in my kids' shoes, really viewing life from their perspective, I would conclude they had been abandoned.

15 You can't hide a penis in a locker room.

16 Bureaucracies are the bane of democracies.

17 When I am manic, the best thing I can do is shut my mouth.

18 I usually don't realize that others might be as sensitive and screwed up as I am.

19 Overstimulation leads to intense irritability.

20 If you're going to get freaky, you had better be good at it.

21 Nature: if I kill it, I won't be able to enjoy it or use it when I need it.

22 When inexperienced riders start driving the bus, there might be a problem.

23 Million-Buck Bill loves endorphins; it just takes a toll getting them.

24 When you die, you are either with the Lord or you are not. It's that painfully simple.

25 Most of my life is an embarrassment, in the rearview window.

26 If you are with a woman getting jiggy with it, and you are not proud of her, then stop getting jiggy.

27 My friend's comment regarding my taking an online quiz: "That's why it was a five-minute quiz you took. The publishers didn't want to delve into the mindset of a pony-tailed, redneck, philosopher, who shoots up small fishponds and slays little does, while under the influence of rye and weed."

28 I have no "bidness" in show "bidness."

29 I want to live in the present, if I can control it.

30 If the Lord's Word is a lamp unto my feet, then I better turn the light on.

31 Chat with a fella about himself and he'll listen incessantly.

32 The second mile is always longer than the first one.

33 Getting to Heaven doesn't depend on whiskey.

34 If you are going to "knock up," you better step up.

35 The center of the universe is not always at the center, and it surely is not in the middle.

36 If this is not me, then I don't know who I am.

37 God speaks to me; I don't always understand Him, but that is not His fault.

38 When it comes to family, telling the Truth is not always the best option.

39 Better to stay silent than to speak and be petty.

40 It's easy not to care about folks who are dismissive of you when you are not forced to be around them.

41   "Why not rather be wronged" is a tough enough mantra to think about, but an even tougher taskmaster when tested.

42   The Lord and I have been tussling over something, but I'm afraid I don't have Jacob's stamina.

43   If Jesus's own family didn't appreciate Him, then I have no reason to court recognition.

44   Forgiving others "seventy times seven" times is a lot, but it wasn't a suggestion.

45   If we force someone to choose, we've already lost.

46   Family is one of the most "rated" entities: underrated when catastrophe hits; overrated when the good times lend to easy judgment and no affirmation.

47   Silence can be as excoriating as being incessantly berated.

48   The stuff that gets you is the internal stuff that keeps showing back up. Only God.

49   Hopefully with the rain comes the pledge of a good conscious toward the things of God.

50   There's alone, then there's ALONE; I'm just alone.

51   I have a thin, microscopic thread of selfish brilliance, God-given; the rest of my thinking is my fault.

52   The reality in my head—though real—is not always the same as what's around me.

53   Paper-thin skin can be shredded by words, or even the lack of them.

54   Occluding fog enhances what's nearby.

55 The immediacy of world news upsets me, and I have plenty on my plate as it is.

56 I am too fragile to stick around if I am not wanted.

57 At times I am thankful when depression hits me—and it does too often without warning—as I tumble in my minnow's version of the belly of Jonah's whale, grasping brief moments of appreciation and recognition of God's amenities and favor.

58 I am always more comfortable turning counterclockwise.

59 If things bother me and I can't seem to shrug them off, then in reflecting on them so often, I'm not so sure it helps.

60 Lord, please protect me wherever I am, 'cause I don't really know where I am.

61 Cycles come and go; maybe that's why they call them cycles—they just keep coming around even when you think the wheel may have finally stopped.

62 We cry for innocence lost; yet we keep shredding it with behaviors birthed in youth and abuse.

63 I never remember, literally, what I write, so it would behoove me to tell the truth.

64 I can't bear the pain in the knowing and reckoning of innocents out there who are being treated in ways the vivid memory never will forget; yet I fear I care too little.

65 Only God makes sense to one so unaccustomed to making sense.

66 The world is raw for the sensitive fella trying to pull off wearing big-man clothes.

67. I feel as though I am back, though first-buzz mania has a way of fooling me.

68. I can't juggle anything.

69. I seem to write more when I realize how messed up I am.

70. Not all elephants in the graveyard are dead.

71. What just took me down for a few days might have produced a little fruit.

72. Sometimes you don't see the fog until you turn on the bright lights.

73. Everybody in my life outgrows me quickly.

74. I should always extend grace to others who don't play well with others because I don't play well with others.

75. Coming home can be a good thing, but it gets harder the longer you are there.

76. I don't like to be guilt-tripped; I'm already full of it.

77. The problem with writers who rarely write is they never really deal with the issues they need to write about.

78. I've finally realized that darkness, like the persistent thorn in the Apostle Paul's side, will never leave me alone for long. Only God.

79. When I shy away, slink away or downright hide, I think I am protecting others and myself.

80. I love—crave—solitude, but if left too long alone, my self gets pretty "squirrelly."

81. I'm always looking for credit and all that implies.

82   I like high water until I get wet.

83   Christians who can't be nice when you've said, "I'm sorry" are missing the very boat Jesus commanded them to fish from as they cast their nets.

84   The good thing about the Elephant's Graveyard—if one makes it—is he or she has chosen where to die.

Chapter 3

1. Holding court feels good when the room is attentive.

2. Social-justice warriors should only pursue such in a democratic society if they are prepared to give up all they have for what they deem a great cause.

3. Sadly, when others emote, it bothers me; when I emote, it seems to make sense...to me, anyway.

4. If God & Guns doesn't make sense to others, then I don't need to get angry; I just need to inform.

5. For all I know, the person smiling at me may be picturing blowing my head off, but it's best to think the best.

6. My valuing others should not be contingent upon them valuing me, but it usually is.

7. I trust people who really trust the Lord; I just need to do a better job trusting Him myself.

8. I like being alone; it's alienation I can't stand.

9. Folks, who I assume hate me, don't spend as much time thinking about me as I assume.

10. One cannot stick me in a hornet's nest and not expect me to swat at some stuff.

11. Those who browbeat the doers end up with nothing to do when the doers take their toys & taxes elsewhere.

12. One thing about technology is it gave me a voice no one wants to hear.

13 The people who can really do one the most wrong usually won't.

14 My brain can't keep up with my brain; makes me insane.

15 Self is a harsh teacher.

16 Thankfully, children lost may never know the pain of adulthood.

17 I don't need to feed my iconoclastic crusader.

18 I like my own company; I usually always agree with myself.

19 When I'm looking down on others, there are plenty of others looking down on me.

20 If it were easy, then I reckon it wouldn't be real.

21 I don't really leave when I'm gone, but I still don't know where I am when I get there.

22 I need to seek a better awareness of the Lord's attention, as He is always attentive.

23 All a man wants in a woman is a gentle spirit, a pretty face, sweet breath and some pretty awesome hygiene. Well, that's a start.

24 If I'm awake, I'm working, in my head.

25 If I looked at the misfortune of all others as if it were my own kids' misfortune, then I would be infinitely more Christ-like in my overall demeanor.

26 How could I possibly ever be whole short of eternity?

27 Maintaining distinctions matters.

28 I live in a world where smell matters.

29 Ask me if I have a son and I'll say I don't know.

30 I "think" I create my best stuff when high.

31 All I do is make the Truth more interesting.

32 I can't live without a trigger.

33 When my brain floods, I just got to let the silt settle.

34 Everyone is on the margins somewhere, and if not, then he or she hasn't left the center of the box.

35 It's amazing how so many talented people are so incredibly ignorant.

36 I definitely ride the emotional short bus.

37 I try to work just enough not to be depressed with too much thinking time; just enough works for me.

38 I'm really just a scared rabbit in a big bunny suit.

39 I can go from worm to glow worm and back to worm before quick.

40 You can't accomplish much if you are not a little messed up.

41 I ride an emotional unicycle.

42 Just because Christians mess up, often, does not mean the world is any less accountable to God.

43 Being contrary in nature can be worse than being an alcoholic.

44 Hashtag is the new rag.

45 I have gotten worked up over something that has not even happened…yet.

46 Sometimes you have to cross a boundary line to know where it is.

47 They don't call it the Crossroads for no reason.

48 To really appreciate the New Testament, a familiarity with the Old Testament matters.

49 I remember best what I talk about often.

50 I too often give impressions, not empiricism.

51 I hate I share my dysfunction with others, yet I do.

52 If it's in our hearts to really do others good, then we don't have to worry so much about our actions.

53 Life & whiskey: I don't use a jigger; I just pour 'til it feels right.

54 Cool will kill cool quickly if being cool matters...be yourself; that's cool.

55 One day something we do will "go viral," and it might be awesome...for less than a moment.

56 Concerning hats, what a person wears on his or her head makes a statement, even if it doesn't.

57 There are those who never stop talking years off your life.

58 Bureaucracies with little accountability accomplish little.

59 Is the Gospel offending them, or am I?

60 Intelligence unchallenged leads to serious debilitation.

61 Mediocrity wins every time bureaucracies are not held accountable, and they rarely are.

62   If you get high long enough, you will eventually throw things out of a closed window.

63   "Kind of busy" works for me.

64   You know you're high when you ransack the car looking for the keys in the ignition.

65   I like capitalizing the word Favor. God's Favor matters.

66   It's hard to get off the full-tilt boogie once it starts.

67   Overstimulation via too many choices is like smelling too much perfume—one gets a headache.

68   Vain janglers' jangling always ends.

69   The Prodigal is not always the youngest.

70   I fear I will not die well.

71   I bet Jesus never calls me "retarded" when I act like it.

72   If I can choose to make a good decision, then actually make it, my life will change demonstrably.

73   When I write dark stories, in my head or on paper, I often wonder, does it take me to a dark place or just evidence where I am?

74   Shooting a sick animal is painful, but it can be necessary.

75   When evening "falls the veil," memory matters most.

76   Distant horizons are a permeable wall.

77   The most noticeable carrot is often the smallest.

78   Reapers reap, sowers sow.

79 When people begin a statement with "to be honest with you" it usually means they are buying time to figure out how to appear honest.

80 I am happiest just being.

81 Carpetbaggers and scalawags rarely say thank you.

82 I'm not smart, because I think I'm smart.

83 Carpetbaggers steal more than money. They are like skinwalkers, pilfering souls.

84 If you don't believe perfect people are perfect, just ask them; it's always the fault of someone else.

85 It's emotionally exhausting for the hypersensitive to get soft, then hard, then soft again. Only God.

86 I pretty much think and write stupid stuff all the time.

87 There is no balm for not forgiving other than forgiveness.

88 I hate how tender I get right before getting mean, because I'm mad about being so tender, then tender about being so mean.

Chapter 4

1. A good redemptive story should make one deal with some stuff.

2. There's nothing too big for God to make right.

3. Crucibles crush, but if God is the forger, then new life can emerge.

4. I often wear a mask; I'm just not able to see it.

5. Balancing humors, even for a "mixologist," is a necessary but unwieldy proposition.

6. Elmer Gantry is among us.

7. Religion sells more than religion. True religion markets God only.

8. God commands us to esteem others higher than ourselves; however, it is easier to value those who value us, but it's still a command to value them regardless of what we think of them.

9. Mania and sadness are my constant companions.

10. Peace is my grease, and if I don't have grease, I lock up like a dry motor.

11. I get overloaded easily. The camel's last straw weighs hard upon me.

12. I am more fool than not.

13. I'm a reformed Scotch drinker, having switched to bourbon years ago.

14. One thing leads to another, and then there you are.

15   I've already had my Warhol 15 minutes of fame. I'm ready to go to ground. There is entirely too much stimulation in today's fast-paced, techno-specific, social-media-frenzied Zeitgeist world for a simple Delta philosopher with very limited emotional means. STOP THE WORLD; I WANT TO GET OFF!

16   In the work world, I enjoy wearing different hats, but if required to change them too often or too quickly, I find my head overexposed.

17   I think I've been just smart enough my whole life to pull off jobs I wasn't mentally or emotionally capable of, but it gets more difficult daily to continue the ruse.

18   Just when I think I'm okay, I'm not.

19   I'm a sucker for a sweet spirit every time.

20   I'm a pragmatic idealist who operates more as an apologist.

21   Talking crap for me is not like brain surgery, but dealing with crap is.

22   I am my own "influencer," for good or ill.

23   Writing that works just sneaks up on a fella.

24   The strong will always have land until the meek inherit it from the Strongest.

25   Everybody picks his or her nose, some more delicately and less publicly than others.

26   Tourism is like farming; it's seasonal—all or nothing.

27   All I ever wanted to do was raise my children; I didn't get to.

28   My attention could not span a dry, creek bed.

29 I loathe my weakness, but weakness loathed is not weakness overcome.

30 My accepting forgiveness often seems to be contingent upon my extending the same to others.

31 Longtime professing Christians who won't forgive—even things not needing forgiveness—astound me.

32 Complicated human cats don't have nine lives; it just seems like it.

33 A simple painting can convey as much intellectual and emotional info as a volume of books, so why do some preachers orate lengthy sermons when all we might need is a picture painted well?

34 Some people know the Lord because they don't know not to; that is likely a good thing.

35 I'm dangerous if I get an audience.

36 Peripatetic souls need not be confined.

37 I just think I'm the center of attention because that's the world I live in.

38 I'm tone deaf, but I dig some percussion.

39 It's dangerous to get to thinking I am more important than I am.

40 She may not be effusive, but she's stable.

41 I've been flying a little too close to the sun lately. Prometheus I am not.

42 I'm thankful my mistakes are sifted through God's loving fingers.

43 The only time I complain about insurance is when I don't need it.

44 The noose I too often slip around my neck is sufficient; I don't need another one.

45 I really screwed up yesterday; I think I need to wait a day or two until I think I am once again sufficient to judge others for what I just did.

46 The only cure for intense mania is periodic depression.

47 I've got to quit assuming that people who irritate me are pieces of dung.

48 Wardens can be hard, unforgiving people, even senior ones.

49 The altitude adjustment from my lows to my highs and back again to my lows leaves me dizzy.

50 I am not flying as close to the sun as I was, but I have not quite cleared its orbit.

51 If I can't be myself, then I don't want to ever meet anybody again.

52 You don't know much about my journey, and I don't know much about yours.

53 Telephones and electronic devices should never be utilized during dinner and dialogue—they have irrevocably altered the depth of communication.

54 Wagon ruts are not made for exploration beyond the predictable.

55 I am constantly amazed at successful people who can't figure out if the door doesn't open or lock when turning the key to the left that maybe turning it to the right might just do the trick.

56 I wish I better understood why do I have to fly so close to the sun.

57 It's tiring to go from king to pauper to king and always back to pauper in no time flat.

58   I'm equal parts Oliver Twist and Artful Dodger.

59   Things that are surreal often make sense of the mundane.

60   Majorities who were once minorities who hide behind minority status always confound me.

61   I do not suffer fools gladly, and coming from a fool, that is saying something.

62   As a rule, big-money weddings do not bring out the best in the principals—"self-centeredness" is not lacking.

63   I am an inefficient salesman, because I don't want you to buy anything you don't want, unless it's the Gospel, and that's still between you and God.

64   Dealing with high-maintenance, self-centered guests, given my fractured persona, is as difficult for me as reading mechanical instructions in Arabic—a language I do not know.

65   The rotational spin of the modern world leaves me constantly fractured and confused.

66   It seems many of my guests are allergic to everything except a deep discount.

67   For someone who spends an inordinate amount of time head clearing, I sure am not very good at it. Maybe that's why I have to do it so often.

68   I have an affinity for other folks overwhelmed by technology.

69   Everything overwhelms me.

70   Simple men should never fly close to the sun. The unflappable trajectory overwhelms.

71 Folks think your life is all gravy when all they see is your smile made public.

72 I should not take strong people's strength for granted, because their strength is usually predicated on hard, difficult choices.

73 Sometimes I feel like Frankenstein; the transitions are not sublime.

74 Too busy is like going to a large concert, where intimacy is lost.

75 I flew too close to the sun today; there has to be a better way to deal with mania.

76 If you can't control the monkey, then the monkey controls you.

77 If there were no dark valleys, then there surely wouldn't be any peaks.

78 Sadly, the only prescription sometimes for a "young Turk" socialist is a jingoist who is not scared.

79 The biggest battle is in my head.

80 My discursive behavior—survival-oriented and intrinsic—leaves me floundering but acutely aware.

81 I think I have emotional COPD; depression makes every breath difficult.

82 Thank you, Lord, for the things I am unaware of...

Chapter 5

1. I seem to always fail others, myself, and surely God by not being closer to Him.

2. I'm helpless to help helpless people; that doesn't speak well for me.

3. When I really pray for peace, sometimes it takes a while, not because God doesn't extend it immediately, but my inability to receive it delays its administration.

4. I know I'm exhausting, particularly when I resist growing up.

5. I need to quit looking at intended obstacles through a magnifying glass.

6. Since I can't fake being at peace, then it behooves me to make peace with the Prince of Peace.

7. The only thing that matters is loving the Lord.

8. The only time bullying is acceptable is when bullying a bully, or is it?

9. When I said I was as sober as a judge, I didn't say which judge.

10. Sometimes unction is from God, and sometimes it is just unction.

11. Sadly, it doesn't take much to irritate me.

12. I need to see obstacles as opportunities to be nice.

13. When I think and write, my thoughts are like a sand painting: here for a moment, then gone with the next good breeze.

14. God disciplines those He loves; He loves me, and His discipline is gentle compared to what I deserve.

15. Living in the "present" is difficult for me, but it beats the life I too often craft without God's guidance.

16. If God is good all the time, and He is, then I must accept what comes as having been sifted through His loving arms.

17. Bureaucrats laud bureaucrats. That's what they do.

18. "Be thankful not proud" is a mantra I should heed.

19. It isn't the blues; it's the intimacy.

20. I got to be myself today, and that's a good thing.

21. Good manners are intrinsic to godliness.

22. Gracious and kind are not necessarily synonymous.

23. Living in unrecognizable bubbles stifles more than we realize.

24. It's easy to take people who have a lot of faith for granted and not to realize their faith may not come easily.

25. Once you juxtapose peripatetic ideologies, you get plenty of cognitive dissonance.

26. When my head gets full of too much thinking, classical music sometimes does the trick.

27. I don't want to test God, yet I do.

28. I'm as scared as I've ever been, and I am in as good a place as I've ever been.

29. I hate that I tap dance.

30 If fear of the Lord is the beginning of wisdom, and perfect love casts out fear, then they aren't the same fears.

31 I have a bad habit of being irresponsible.

32 I hate the extremes of my neediness.

33 Sadly, I too often forget I'm not the only one with problems.

34 Some folks just out talk my attention span.

35 I can't predict when I'm going to hit the wall. I just hit it.

36 I often excel at being tired.

37 Eternity will not let me take this hate with me.

38 I don't have the stomach for controversy.

39 Flexibility gets more difficult as I age.

40 I lack empathy because I'm selfish, yet I feel acutely the alienation of the alienated.

41 When I merely glance at solo walkers possessing a distant gaze, I can scarcely breathe imagining their loneliness.

42 Only God understands the inexplicable pit in my stomach.

43 When I scratch my dog, I often think about how many kids never get what he gets: attention, love and an "atta boy or girl!"

44 Humility should be the response of a fool.

45 Patterns matter.

46 With the right heart, just one slice of a Mandarin orange is manna.

47 God's good to us. He is.

48 The things that come out of my mouth when I'm manic are frightening, often offensive, yet occasionally brilliant.

49 At times I wither when observing people humbling themselves, because I know what it is to be humbled.

50 Just because something doesn't work out the way others think it should, does not make one foolish.

51 Some people question every change in your life as if it's always a bad thing.

52 I can be caustic when challenged.

53 When expected relationships aren't deep, sarcasm often rules the day.

54 Just because I haven't shed the control issues I inherited doesn't mean I am not responsible for shedding them.

55 Those raised by controlling parents need eventually to realize as adults that what others think about them is not worth the angst it creates.

56 I am not dependent upon the capricious whims of others for my daily bread.

57 When I'm not reading, I'm usually not mentally stable.

58 I've always felt like an impostor in this world.

59 It's not amazing that God loves me, given who He is; it's just amazing that He loves me.

60 The appropriate answer is always, "Well, we didn't' expect to be invited."

61 Sometimes, I think I just need to get stoned to deal with not being able to deal with something.

62 I know my wife is always praying for God to bring the right folks across our path, and I do too, but I have a hard time not wanting to thin God's herd a bit. He knows. I don't.

63 I don't know that my memory is bad; I think I just need a new starter on my recall button.

64 Sometimes being a housekeeper is easier than being an innkeeper, because linen is silent.

65 My highs may be higher than most folks, but my lows are too.

66 I am always heading home via the back way.

67 Sometimes putting the band back together exemplifies what got you sideways in the beginning.

68 Sometimes I'm scared of my own self.

69 Just because I didn't get to do something shouldn't mean others shouldn't enjoy it.

70 I have the affectations of the tortured artists just not the gifting.

71 Few people work as much as they say they do; even fewer sleep as little as they say they do; and all fall short of the glory of God.

72 Maybe I would be better off focusing on what I don't know instead of what I think I know.

73 I've seen few folks look as far down at the marginalized as do the elite who philosophically and verbally express grand concern.

74 If love is centered on an object, but not based on the actions of that object, then it is likely True Love.

75 Uniformity makes sense and saves space in a congested world, but it can be stifling when thwarting creativity.

76 I've never met anyone cool or good enough to define what constitutes normal.

77 A danger in too much praise is the likelihood that the recipient begins thinking he or she is Teflon.

78 I have a hard time staying between the lines.

79 No two masters think and act the same, so if you have two of them, it's likely going to be a problem.

80 I don't so much nap to get some sleep, but to let my worm-like synapses settle down a bit.

81 Loneliness is one of the greatest behavioral drivers.

82 There will always be bad news.

83 If a man doesn't know his limitations, then the ball is not likely to bounce in his favor.

84 I never understood grace until I really needed it.

85 My multitasking is like pouring hot coffee into a saucer while sneezing incessantly.

86 My lack of peace resides in my mind, and there it must be rectified.

87 I need to go fishing and all that doesn't entail.

Chapter 6

1. I'm not ready to die, but I am thankful I have only one sin-stained life to bear down here.

2. It's hard to be confident when you're knowingly sinning.

3. People who beat you down, then beat you down for being beat down, need a beat down; or, better yet a prayer.

4. Dream "squelchers" squelch what keeps us alive.

5. I'm still underwater, but dry as a bone.

6. He may be smarter than I, but he doesn't know the Lord, and that is his disadvantage.

7. Our relationships are limited by our judgments.

8. If I didn't care, I wouldn't be angry.

9. It's human nature to want more.

10. I have an aversion to the marketplace, not a fear of it.

11. If I'm going to be a fool, and I am, then I need to be God's own fool.

12. When it's time to go, I have got to go.

13. Customer service is becoming more difficult as those being served become increasingly less content with life.

14. Some people need two septic systems for the refuse in their neck.

15. My cup gets filled entirely too quickly.

16   Folks who live on the fringes prefer solitude.

17   When I am weary, all my biggest heartaches come rushing back in like flood waters on a hard, dry plain.

18   When wound too tight, the eventual unwinding is painful.

19   The descent from mania is always too rapid.

20   What some people see as foolish, I see as my greatest accomplishment, with God's help.

21   Lord, please give me the grace to be gracious.

22   Pity affects us; self-pity kills us.

23   If somebody doesn't apologize for a known offense, it just might mean they are pretty pleased with themselves.

24   "Misty, water-colored memories of the way things were" will break a sensitive man with a gelatinous spine.

25   I loathe my deep-seated neediness.

26   A problem with not strictly following one of two herds is both herds will trample the outlier.

27   The nozzle filling my emotional vessel is a fire hose; my vessel fills too quickly.

28   What are shallow scars to some are bottomless crevasses to the sensitive.

29   Scripturally speaking, everybody does not go to heaven.

30   I'm cycling right now, for what that is worth.

31 I can go from wanting to kill myself to king of the world in one second flat.

32 It truly amazes me how easily folks make peace with impending death.

33 Weed does not make me stupid; it reminds me of stuff I forgot, which makes me stupid.

34 I'm not tough enough to talk crap often, ever.

35 I'm not a joiner because I don't want to pick sides in a losing battle.

36 Music is a mystery to me, a foreign language; I only hear the beauty, while not understanding the chemistry.

37 It's never hard to find something wrong with anything.

38 I don't fake well, even when trying.

39 I'm the guy you don't marry. I never quite materialize.

40 Just because I have issues doesn't mean I'm always wrong.

41 Even on my best days, I struggle with sanity.

42 God does not sow discord.

43 I spend an inordinate amount of time avoiding things that might have me say, "to heck with it."

44 Men without God are hollow on the inside; stuff and fame don't bring peace and happiness.

45 I may not understand it or be able to explain it, but God surely does and can.

46 I don't need to worry about my fellow man, except how to better love him.

47 When tired, I either get mean or tender—sometimes both.

48 When mentally exhausted and overstimulated, I often even things out with physical exhaustion.

49 Sometimes we love deeply what we rebel against fiercely.

50 Odds are I'll eventually offend you.

51 How can there be design without a Designer?

52 The more we are denied something, the better it tastes.

53 Idealism can produce egalitarianism until the bubble bursts.

54 I put a lot of stuff on the shelf—even good stuff—until I'm ready to deal with it, if ever.

55 I do have some mental illness; reckon I always have…without God, I would not be okay.

56 Life, at its best, is not a magic carpet ride.

57 I like "au naturale" without the sand and the sticky.

58 I may present well but not be well; or, I may not present well, but be well. Oh, well.

59 One of the problems of being too old is I don't have the time or energy to rectify a lifetime of wrongs. Thankfully, God forgives.

60 If we don't understand the simple, then the complicated won't make sense.

61   There's been a lot of thick and thin in my life, and I created most of the thin.

62   I need to shut up and deal with my own sins and shortcomings.

63   Opening my mouth publicly about things I perceive need rectifying is like going into battle. I had better be prepared, and I am not.

64   I always assume everyone's mind runs at the same speed as mine, but it just is not so, whether fast or slow.

65   I'm usually seconds away from hollow.

66   Divides widen. That's what they do.

67   God is bigger than my mental illness.

68   I'm never okay until I am.

69   There are two ways we are ourselves: one in front of others and one by ourselves. The latter speaks the most truth.

70   I think crazy stuff all the time; maybe that's why I am depressed.

71   The truest things she ever said were foul.

72   I'm like a red-winged blackbird; I like being on the tallest stalk in a flat field of row crops where I can see all…then chirp about it.

73   To boycott anything is a personal decision—not always healthy as groupthink, even if it's effective.

74   Always go overboard; God will bless.

75   Envy is misery.

76   I'll not be whole 'til Heaven.

77 If the process is foul, the product will be too.

78 One cannot fight a Hun or a Khan with the Marquess of Queensberry Rules.

79 The continuous rise and fall of man's favor is precipitous.

80 The devil whispers, "End it all: you abandoned your children, you gutless, pathetic, egocentric weakling." He's right! Lord help me.

81 I have so much, yet I'm so messed up.

82 Every utterance is a cry for help.

83 From high to low doesn't take me but a minute.

84 Contrarian Agrarian Riparian Prelapsarians work as hard as they have to, but no harder than they have to.

Chapter 7

1. I try not to crap on people on Friday afternoons or Sunday evenings; I've too often been the recipient.

2. Smart just isn't enough.

3. A problem with "crazy" is that it never stops.

4. God doesn't have hang-ups or issues. I do. That's one good reason I need him, always.

5. Every tour is the same, just different.

6. How can a robot deal with repentance?

7. All that crap from yesterday, I think I'll deal with tomorrow.

8. Every tour takes a lot out of me, because it takes a piece of me every time.

9. Heaven is God's steady presence.

10. The less I show off, the less vulnerable I feel.

11. Everybody does something different for crazy.

12. I have the attention span of a thirsty mosquito.

13. One of my biggest problems is I don't listen to God.

14. When I think I'm right, I'm often wrong.

15. Some of the most messed-up folks I know are Christians, like me.

16. Oh, the travails of a narcissistic worm.

17 Sometimes, I just need to close my eyes and stare at the ceiling.

18 One song can suck half a day's life out of me.

19 Too much magic makes a man go mad.

20 I can't carry the weight of my children's struggles. They are my fault, yet I am too weak to bear them.

21 I'm a terrible father.

22 There is no depth deeper than lonely and shame.

23 There is no Gipper.

24 Depression is exhausting, even in abeyance.

25 When I'm deeply depressed—not an anomaly—I just want people who love me to just love me, to give me time and space to deal with me, while still being supportive by not making me feel more depressed for being depressed.

26 I would not wish being married to me on anyone.

27 I'm under water more than most realize, but prefer being on the water, not under it. Sometimes it is what it is, and the hope of "on" makes the "under" bearable, with God's help.

28 Man, I sure can see other people's mess-ups. Mine? Not so deeply or intently.

29 Can't even write a letter to my daughter in my head without thinking about publishing it. What is my problem? If I make it universal, maybe I think I am avoiding responsibility on an individual level.

30. I could be offered the whole world and every good thing in it for eternity, but I wouldn't want it, as it would be hollow shortly after reception if God wasn't doing the giving and in charge of it.

31. Sometimes, saying it keeps me from doing it.

32. The Rabbit Hole is dark and hollow.

33. The problem with sharing depression with loved ones is they can't help but offer good solutions with good intentions, but often it makes the depressed more depressed because we are too depressed to enact them.

34. I love her because she hurts like I do.

35. Depression doesn't necessarily end because it ends.

36. It's hard to feel loved, by anybody, when depressed.

37. Feelings of disappointment by loved ones are painful when depressed.

38. Sometimes I get tired of asking God for help, even if it has only been a few minutes. I should not treat Him as if He is at my beck and call.

39. No one, not even loved ones, can truly understand or be there for me when I'm depressed. I alone am responsible for my depression and the hopeful elimination of it, at least in the short run. Only God.

40. I am not tough enough to judge anybody or anything.

41. Being right doesn't necessarily make it right.

42. I write viscerally, often masking the truth in the name of Truth, when I really should not write at all.

43. Sadly, I must want people to say, "Poor Malachi," without saying it publicly.

44 Art is often just someone's pain made manifest.

45 I often, particularly when upset, think people who are close to me and disagree with me are implying they are not on my team.

46 I take out my weaknesses on others.

47 I don't seem to be able to bear my own depression, much less the depression of others likely caused by me.

48 I made my bed; I just didn't have the tenacity to lie in it.

49 Depression is a lonely walk, on so many levels.

50 I hope I really mean it when I say I'm tired of conning God, others, and myself.

51 The post-depression blues is a rabbit hole; it's just not as deep as the depths of depression. It has more light, yet movement is still slow or non-existent; it's like a halfway house to better.

52 I'm always surprised when people love me, even when I arrogantly assume they already do.

53 This last bout of depression surprised and scared me maybe more than any before.

54 Taking a bath after coming out of a major depressive episode is as much an act of faith as it is an act.

55 It's an incredible feeling to be at peace once again, even if just for a season.

56 I am thankful for His words. They inspire. In writing, I can often squeeze out some things I press down that come out sideways when I don't.

57 I live within the confines of my mind; it's time to branch out.

58 I think what scared me the most about this last depression was I couldn't think my way out of it.

59 Balance requires me to choose where to lend-not-rend my energy.

60 I require that too many things have meaning.

61 I should not ridicule what I don't understand.

62 I can write only what I feel.

63 There is little more effective in getting rid of depression—momentarily only—than getting mad at someone.

64 She's smarter than anybody I know because she listens to God; she really listens.

65 Famous last words by a cliff jumper: "Hey Man, I just wanted to make a difference."

66 If I'm not at peace with loved ones with whom I am in a relationship, then I am not okay.

67 I'm my biggest problem.

68 The devil whispers too; we just shouldn't listen. Only God.

69 While we get much self-esteem from working, our self-worth should not be based on a job.

70 Death is a big deal.

71 Though I am the most messed up person I know, it doesn't mean I'm always wrong.

72 I just feel raw and exposed right now—too scared to live, too scared to die.

73 I hate smartphones; they have ruined the world.

74 Sometimes I just want to not feel insane; maybe by creating art associated with those considered insane, I can feel differently.

75 Erudite fluff cajoles me.

76 Iconoclasts may not live long, but they do get things moving.

77 I am proof crazy folks get to Heaven.

78 Even a placebo can be therapeutic.

79 Commonalities are found in authenticity.

80 Divorce equals death.

81 I'm going to end up crazy, if I'm not already.

82 I've been a fool my whole life; now I'm paying for it with my life.

83 Hey man, I don't have a clue if I am all right.

84 Even the good life can exhaust the depressed.

85 When deeply depressed, I feel like my chest is slowly but surely imploding.

86 Deep depression makes me want to sleep until I miraculously feel better, or Eternity arrives.

87 Finally, today, I really admitted to my wife and myself that I need help. I have been depressed for probably five weeks now, and it is not going to get better on its own. I've got to get some help. Lord, please help me!

Chapter 8

1. For somebody who doesn't like physical masks, I sure do wear a lot of immaterial ones.

2. I should treat others who have treated me poorly as if they just treated me splendidly.

3. Deeply, deeply depressed and life has no flavor: TV, booze, weed, pills, reading, walking, eating, sex, sleep, all offer no relief for this constant, constant, constant, nervous, debilitating, paralyzing hopelessness.

4. I feel like I'm holding my breath under water…can't hold it forever, or even much longer. Lord, please help me?

5. I'll try to stay the course until I can't…which is a real possibility…it's just tragic that it takes so little to overwhelm me.

6. Pre-treatment: 9/10/18: God hears the thoughts of those who don't know Him, too; they mean a lot to this fallen, little man, who thankfully does know Him, yet serves Him and others so poorly.

7. Post treatment: 10/17/18: The disease rages within, always promoting sin, due to the devil's kin, I've already lost a friend.

8. Do I need Wisdom or humility more? Hmmm? I need Wisdom to have and understand humility, and I need humility to understand and have Wisdom—both impossible without God.

9. Life is a phase.

10. The Jordan River runs through the Elephant's Graveyard.

11. It's not worth the gamble; all gamblers lose.

12 The largest of government and those who support it because of wanting votes or because of guilt have crippled people on the margins in the name of goodwill.

13 My desire is to be fruitful this winter, even during a time of predictable dormancy. God is able.

14 I realize I will always have to deal with addiction issues and depression. The bad news is I'll always have to deal with them; the good news is I can deal with them.

15 Cheesy sayings bother me, unless I thought of them first.

16 Human nature unchecked internally by a loving God, nor externally checked by a system based on His principles, is a frightening thing.

17 I no longer refer to myself as an addict as being a pejorative, but as recognition of the recognition of which keeps me aware of my condition helping me to stay clean and sober and self-reflective about the things I need to work on.

18 Truth is not hard to quote; it's hard to live. And with that statement, I incriminate myself.

19 Don't say "sorry;" be sorry, then quit acting sorry.

20 Until we admit we are helpless to control anything, we can't get help from anybody.

21 We should not bite the hand that feeds us unless we are prepared to feed ourselves.

22 War, even a just and necessary one, robs each person of some of his or her humanity.

23 I go crazy when with company; I go mad when I'm alone.

24 Leisure without purpose can be rather exhausting.

25 A bridge burned cannot be mended until the torchbearer has surrendered.

26 You might be an addict if you threw up the best meal you ever had.

27 Alienation is difficult, but infinitely rich, if pursued artistically. If the custodial parent is not supportive of the non-custodial parent, then the non-custodial parent will always be viewed as an interloper.

28 Why do I struggle so; maybe, so I'll know I need God!

29 I'm thankful for almost sanity; without it I might not reach out to God.

30 People change everyday, yet hardly at all.

31 We can't change others to make them happy, and we aren't going to change them to make us happy.

32 Things that matter are hard for me to deal with, because they do matter and fear of failure sets in.

33 Without a belief in God the thought of nothingness is more peaceful than a painful life. The problem? I don't believe there is "nothingness" afterwards; either there is awesomeness forever, or eternity unimaginable.

34 As I age and life grinds on me, I become more aware of things that scar and things that heal.

35 If I write for affirmation, I will always be disappointed.

36 Getting high: short-term gain, long-term pain.

37 Even the good life is difficult for a fella like me who too often lives deep within his head.

38 Without books, my life would tend toward the lonely and dull.

39 For good or ill, we all pretty much act like we were raised.

40 Don't assume someone has not tried to make amends just because you see no evidence of them.

41 Amazing how people try to be hip by appearing not to be hip.

42 The reason I'm okay is that I know I'm not.

43 My head is my most profound antagonist, but it sure is easier to reckon with clean and sober.

44 Just because I sadly used others does not mean I have to let others use me in Recovery.

45 Memories are painful, even good ones, because they are no more.

46 I'm a tortured artist who can't even draw interest.

47 Water will save a thirsty man's life, if he will drink it.

48 I want to write poetry in the almost vernacular of the common man.

49 Every day that I try to be a better person I am making amends.

50 I hail from just enough society where if everybody in town is invited, I might just make the cut.

51 Just because we have similar ideologies and political views does not mean I necessarily agree with you.

52 Plucking hairs from self is a messed-up man's attempt for stability, balance, and sameness.

53 Any higher power can get you clean and sober, but only One can get you into the Eternal presence of God.

54 If someone ever says, "What have you got to be depressed about?" then, they don't deal with depression.

55 When looking in the mirror and trying to compare myself to Tom Cruise, I instantly realize why I need to keep writing in the dark.

56 Almost sanity keeps me calling on God.

57 I'm too quick to believe what I want to hear and too quick to dismiss what I don't want to listen to.

58 My whole life is a stream of unconscious consciousness; before Recovery, it was just the opposite—stream of conscious unconsciousness.

59 Maybe a great poet should not write a novel; maybe a great novelist should not write poetry…maybe.

60 Asking me to help with plumbing is like asking a bon vivant to step in and assist with last-minute brain surgery.

61 If you consistently spout stuff that is not true, then there's something seriously wrong with you.

62 I produce poorly when fettered, yet remarkably well when slightly disturbed.

63 My sanity is not a given, ever.

64 Life is a short ride, and it doesn't take long to get there.

65 Many people would throw away their lives for a quick anything.

66 The days when I live mostly in my head are the days I struggle the most.

67 I didn't know a thing yesterday. Today? Still not so much.

68 Only I can occlude the sun.

69 The wind blows, the sun recedes, and fish are seen no more, yet they remain.

70 I have come to believe that, unlike many perfectionists, I don't procrastinate out of fear of failure; I procrastinate out of fear of movement or change.

71 I am not doing well today, but I'll be all right.

72 We don't mind folks being limited, as long as they know they're limited.

73 I am not a drummer, but I beat my own drum.

74 Shall I deny others beauty, because I'm bent out of shape about something else?

75 Living on the edge of a world gone by is suffocating.

76 The only place I am not lazy is inside my head.

77 Money has often bought someone a bigger, grander, lonelier existence.

78 Even with the right meds, there are many days I'm as flat as a thin pancake.

79 When feeling low, it's amazing how gray a colorful landscape can appear.

80 When I am living in my head and depressed, I just assume everybody else is too.

81 Bad memories only have the power to affect me when I let them. And I let them.

82 At times I'm too lazy to even turn the A/C on in the middle of summer.

83 When it's slow, I am depressed; when it's fast, I am stressed; in-between? I regress.

84 Thought complicates things.

85 I remember as a kid how my shoulder blades could almost touch behind me, now they call each other long distance.

86 I mostly dread what's in my head.

87 I've always been hollow.

88 The thoughtfulness of the wounded submitted to God plumbs depths not ventured by the un-scarred.

89 To attack the religion undergirding the freedom to attack religion is foolish.

90 Addiction unchecked trumps "smarts" every time.

Chapter 9

1. At times I'm amazed that anybody likes me and at other times I'm floored everybody doesn't like me.

2. It really isn't my job to judge the entire world.

3. The silent sounds of the Mississippi Delta are my favorite music.

4. Sweet boys do stupid stuff too.

5. When I kayak, I am Riparian, when I walk in the country, I am Agrarian, when I pray I am Prelapsarian.

6. If declarations could stop the wind, Washington, D.C. would be flatulence-free.

7. I don't know what I'm going to do tomorrow, yet I still selfishly try to control tomorrow.

8. Socialism has sensibilities void of sense.

9. My wife tells me she loves me every day; it makes a difference.

10. Lord, let your Spirit speak through me; yet, I still fear the whip, Lord.

11. A few days shy of one year of being drug-free and sober, I'm starting to have brief flashes of healthy mania.

12. I don't ever want to be intoxicated or high again, just in case somebody needs me.

13. The Lord gave me plenty smarts; I've just spent a lifetime using them to get stupid.

14. Humility saves us from a lot of pain and apologies.

15   Just thinking in retrospect about my insane life in active addiction exhausts me.

16   Priorities change when you stop drinking and getting high.

17   Liturgy is meaningful if you mean it.

18   It amazes me when I think about the folks who fooled around on their spouses, who were then vocally dismayed at my wife for taking a picture of me, nude in the snow, with zero privates showing.

19   The Circle of Love celebrates others.

20   Strong-yet-fragile operates best when humble.

21   Too often I do everything I need to do instead of first doing what I need to do.

22   When praying I tend to call the Triune Godhead, "Y'all."

23   Sadly, civilization has wrought an unthankful people who gripe about the very amenities civilization has wrought in abundance.

24   It's clear to me now, saying "I'm sorry" is not making amends, and when making amends to people I've wronged, I need not ever add an excuse or caveat.

25   I can only be a "people person" if I get my non-people-person time alone without overstimulation.

26   I don't remember the details of books, movies and events, but I remember how they made me feel—kind of like people.

27   If God sees His reflection when looking at the Redeemed, then what a beautiful picture He sees.

28   The thought of Hell really disturbs me.

29 Creative types are better at creating what they enjoy…unless they have to make a living from their art.

30 One molecule of feces can stink up a royal rose garden.

31 When I'm thankful, everything is good enough; when I'm unthankful, nothing is good enough.

32 A personal journal does not require perfection. So, write.

33 The addict always thinks he has more time.

34 Many are impressed when you come bearing money; I'm impressed if you bear honey. Be sweet.

35 Life sure is more pleasant when I don't act ugly.

36 When I need a respite, I try to avoid high-maintenance, difficult people. Toxicity erodes.

37 In America, if one has a particular gifting, inclination, work ethic and the right breaks, then he can be anything he wants, though it often takes all four.

38 I saw your gaze today, though not directed my way; I feel your pain as few can—I've been there before. I'm so sorry.

39 Resentments unchecked make me isolate; isolation leads to active addiction.

40 I no longer debate with people who disagree with me politically regarding my long-held beliefs that I believe to be inviolable.

41 I sure can't take credit for why God is so good to me.

42 Justice does not include suing someone just because you can, or because he has money.

43 I don't work well, play well or collaborate well with others; just let me do my thing.

44 Sometimes it's hard to see little children, because I didn't get to raise mine.

45 The greatest 21st-century advancement is our greatest distractor—the smartphone.

46 I'm the toughest marshmallow there ever was.

47 I burn a lot fewer bridges today, but I'm still apt to light one up on occasion.

48 Sometimes, even sober, my head has too much stuff in it.

49 People are drawn to the light even if they don't love it or understand why.

50 Try to put me in a box. I promise I won't fit.

51 Most of the world lives in segregated places, yet many judge the Mississippi Delta as segregated; yet we truly are one of the most diversified, collaborative places on Earth.

52 Only God can forgive sins, yet Jesus did.

53 On fight day, I go South.

54 What happens next matters.

55 If I don't do it now, I probably am not going to do it later.

56 If God is not who He says He is, then I'm in trouble. I am not in trouble.

57 I may be lazy, but at least I get depressed when I do nothing.

58 The next right thing doesn't require a formal start time. Just start.

59 The world cannot see and understand God if they don't want to see and understand God.

60 I wonder what Jesus dreamed about when sleeping.

61 Life for a head-dweller is difficult on a good day.

62 I sure don't seem as depressed when I'm sound asleep.

63 If I don't daily exercise my spirit, body, and mind, I will not be okay.

64 Just 'cause I cleared the trees doesn't mean I'm out of the forest.

65 Living inside my head is too often a gangplank to an abyss.

66 I envy a male dog; he never tires of sleeping, eating, or loving.

67 Voices crying in the Wilderness need to count the cost.

68 Some folks think highly enough of themselves that I don't need to.

69 People are dying near and far, yet I still worry about what others think of me.

70 Life gets busy even when it is not busy.

71 I'm not what I was, because I can't be what I'm not. That is not me.

72 I'm the prodigal who almost made it home.

73 I can be inspired when something is not intrinsically inspirational, and then conversely be uninspired when it is.

74 A key to living successfully in modernity is to enjoy modern amenities while not being distracted by them.

75 Even a bird's brain recognizes the inherent danger in a slow-moving vehicle.

76 If they were expecting a country bumpkin, they didn't get one.

77 I don't always write when depressed, slighted, or marginalized, but I do write because of them.

78 Just because I quote Chesterton doesn't mean I've read Chesterton…yet.

79 Recovery cannot supplant or replace the Church catholic, but it can augment it.

80 I have to write the way my brain thinks; otherwise, it's not authentic, even if it's hard to understand.

81 I've always been too insecure to be an authentic misfit.

82 Little irritates me more than someone who makes me irritable then tells me not to be irritable.

83 I remember a day when what one did in one state did not matter in another state; now, everything matters.

84 We may live in a cruel world, but a cruel God did not create it.

85 I'm always coming down from something.

86 Some of the most dangerous things for a wandering man include lips smooth as oil, sweet breath, a pretty face and a lack of discretion.

87 Asking me to watch mainstream media, which too often pursues specious narratives—so I'll be more open-minded—is akin to asking me as a Christian to read the satanic bible for the same reason.

88 I fear I am too sensitive to be a crier in the Wilderness.

10 Chapter

1. Intellect does not equal reality.

2. A "bondservant to the Present" is where I want to be in the future.

3. Strangely, the immediacy of communication has facilitated the demise of civilization as we know it.

4. I am an egalitarian recovering addict; I drink coffee & tea.

5. There is little that is more dangerous than a coot swimming in front of a bored duck hunter on a flightless day.

6. An upside of daily remembering that I'm an addict is that I daily remember I'm an addict.

7. I don't do buffets; I just can't.

8. I've heard of people who only eat when they are hungry.

9. I'm at home on the water.

10. Addicts and alcoholics don't use jiggers.

11. I would love to sit and talk to myself for a while.

12. If I really knew God, I would be prostrate.

13. I couldn't save a cup of water in a rainstorm.

14. I'm amazed at how often those thought ignorant are right.

15. Broke and happy is when a full humidor is my greatest financial asset.

16. Everything affects me, and at times nothing affects me.

17 There is arrogance in my humility and humility in my arrogance.

18 There are no high-rises in the Delta.

19 Nothing good comes out of an incessantly wandering thought life.

20 I'm a simple philosopher who can't handle too much thinking.

21 I will not be cowed by political antitheses, but I will also not debate them on social media. Peace.

22 Continuity can be stifling, yet it matters.

23 I look forward to not being overstimulated for Eternity; if I am, I know I'll be able to handle it.

24 I'm not enough, never have been.

25 Often the difference between terror and peace is light.

26 I get higher than dope when the sun shines on a warming winter day.

27 I can easily get overwhelmed and overstimulated and never leave my head.

28 Life is usually lived between yes and no.

29 At times, lazy paralyzes me.

30 I think I've always been me; I just am not real sure who I've been.

31 We try to clean the temporal while neglecting the eternal.

32 Socialism always ends with Stalin.

33 I can't base my Faith or my Recovery on how I feel or think at the moment.

34 I'm a relational guy who likes to work alone.

35 I'm having a panic attack right now; I need to start reading the open Bible next to me.

36 I no longer have an active addiction to help me in trying times; all I have is the Lord and the comfort of His Word and Spirit.

37 Some days all I have is being clean, sober, and thankful.

38 Often, the apex of my do-right is "willing to," and that just barely.

39 Vienna sausages are making a comeback in the Howell household.

40 My needful prayer is I will work for my employer as unto the Lord, and that I will better understand and honor what that means.

41 I have not even gotten to work and I'm ready to come home.

42 Some days my mind just sifts through the ashes.

43 The times may be worrisome and the future unknown, but I am thankful that I can pass a piss test.

44 I'm what I unwittingly always dreaded: a 60-year-old job hunter.

45 We should never be surprised by "privilege."

46 In times like these, a decent cigar and a back porch help keep my train on the tracks.

47 If I have learned anything in this complicated life, it should be: "Don't burn any bridges."

48 Cigars might not keep the addict clean, but they sure do help.

49 Life is often hardest in the rearview mirror.

50 There are times I correctly and incorrectly assume I'm the only one, then I correctly and incorrectly realize I'm just one of many.

51 I finally am able to see chipmunks, frogs, turtles and wrens up close when I sit still for a spell.

52 Beds are made and unmade for sleeping, not for hiding.

53 The mind of a wren is solely focused on the next task.

54 Cigars, a pretty day and a back porch still are not enough…only God.

55 Limbo is difficult when you aren't very flexible.

56 Best not to judge any region's sensibilities and peculiarities until better understood.

57 Overqualified is a misnomer; there is just qualified.

58 There is no shame in being an alcoholic, only shame in not doing something about it.

59 Batteries work, if maintained, because they have a positive and a negative charge.

60 I will always be an addict and a sinner; yet, I don't have to live in active addiction.

61 The saying, "We can always come home," is contingent on the home and the homeowner.

62 Too much energy coupled with flattery is exhausting.

63 When I get stressed, I get anxious and depressed; when I get too much relief, I get anxious and depressed.

64 We should not consider ourselves gurus simply because we helped someone.

65 How can a lost world find purpose when told it was not created and that abortion is a legal and viable answer to being unwanted?

66 Doing Godly stuff sure helps with my depression and anxiety.

67 I'll always start tomorrow.

68 If it's good, it's a gift.

69 The problem with jumping off a moving boat into an intoxicating ocean is that you can't take it back.

70 When addicts with edges rub shoulders, it can get a bit prickly at times.

71 I'm too lazy to do anything if I am not "eat up" with it.

72 I can't successfully live in someone else's head when I have so much trouble in my own.

73 When considering the final solution, I'd be better off dying with credit card debt than dying because of it.

74 For the easily overstimulated, overstimulation is the non-physical equivalent of being drawn and quartered.

75 I'm more smart-stupid than stupid-smart.

76 My brain becomes exhausted when I stay awake too long.

77 I've spent my whole life just surviving in the Land of the Free.

78 I've had religion for a while; I'm working on spirituality now.

79 God can use our debt that I've largely created to lovingly guide our future.

80 As long as I don't think about it, I don't think about it.

81 Dogs don't feel guilt, just shame.

82 I may have a disease, but I still sinned in active addiction.

83 Perceived failures are but blips on the learning curve.

84 Peace is unattainable if chaos is the driving wheel.

85 Rioting might make sense to us, until it's damaging to our property.

86 I can't remember what it was, but I remember it was something.

Chapter 11

1. My pseudonyms have pseudonyms.

2. Poetry burns within me.

3. When the marginalized or anyone else is given a reconstructive advantage and we do not take advantage of the advantage, then shame on us.

4. Poetry needs no introduction or explanation.

5. Every new thing is a "fad," but there is "no new thing under the sun;" fads get traction due to the attention we derive from the attention of those who most seek attention.

6. If we cried for the tragic death of children like we lament the tragic death of animals, the world would be a different, fuller place.

7. My poetry seems best articulated when I am affected, yet still not too encumbered to compose.

8. Sometimes we need chicken broth to make chicken broth.

9. My heart is the toughest thing for God to get hold of because He gives me free will.

10. It's for the best for those seeking a release not to gamble.

11. I want to scream right now, but feel God is saying no—maybe because I want to scream.

12. Drinking alcohol did not make me a better person...period.

13. Jealousy and envy are the easiest yet most dangerous emotions.

14   I'll probably start back smoking and drinking if I ever "give up" again.

15   Our politics differ, but he's one of the brightest, dumb fellas I know; hope he would say the same thing about me.

16   I want to be as bold as I'm supposed to be but not as foolish as I am.

17   I recognize Darkness.

18   I may be "sorry," but I recognize those who are not "sorry."

19   It's coming, Civil War; and, just like the first one, no one wins.

20   Recovery took me from smoking in a fireworks stand to dull in a nanosecond, and, two years down the road, I'm okay with that.

21   Two years clean and sober: the monkey may be mostly off my back, but he still daily tries to flag a ride, and if I let him, then he's going to want to drive.

22   I don't read to be well-rounded; I read for enjoyment, and hopefully in that I become well-rounded.

23   God-given and natural gifts come easily; maintaining and sharing them takes work.

24   My goal is to: Think right. Will right. Do right. Write right.

25   I can't memorize what I don't understand.

26   Every day of my life has been a spare.

27   I don't think about not making sense; I just don't make sense.

28   Willfully ignorant equals stupid.

29   I was ranked before I started.

30 I often wonder if I really used to be a good guy or was I just a great conman, likely a combination of both.

31 If it, whatever it is, doesn't produce a positive change in me, then it is not worth doing.

32 My limited empathy sadly does not correlate with my intense sensitivity.

33 I am often judged by the length of my hair. Why does something that brings me so much pleasure, and hurts no one, bother so many people who feel a need to share their unsolicited opinion?

34 I've reached a point in my life where I couldn't even be a Wal-Mart greeter, because I can't stand that long.

35 Irritations make me think, and thinking makes me deal, and dealing makes me choose how I am going to deal with what I am thinking.

36 If I am going to make a splash, then I need to make sure the ripples are righteous.

37 I was not mean when drinking, but I was a bit edgy.

38 Reality includes "trickle down."

39 Self-pity carries more emotion than pity; henceforth, the inherent danger.

40 The specter that tracks me, it's not its fault.

41 Hey man, she's just a selfie girl living in a selfie world.

42 If you ask me, if I am growing my hair long again, you probably already know the answer.

43 Elitism: Precepts and laws apply to you; they don't apply to me and mine.

44 I like talking with her; she listens.

45 I've reached a point in my life where I don't want to kill anything that doesn't need killing.

46 I just can't figure out a way to get around or make peace with social media.

47 Having character includes loving the Truth.

48 Please don't presume to know how a death affects me.

49 Even the good life includes tragedy.

50 Consistently defending a known untruth surely rots the soul.

51 All my thoughts are authentic and original to me, but that doesn't make them original.

52 There are many reasons a relapse ends in a full-tilt boogie.

53 Sometimes a fella has to purpose to have purpose, and then he must act purposefully.

54 A perfect storm sure seems to hit the already sullen during the holidays.

55 Likely, most of my thoughts and words—spoken and unspoken—have always been a cry for help.

56 Thankfulness is a great equalizer and should be the hallmark of a Christian.

57 It's amazing the booze and drugs I used to be able to survive in uncomfortable environs, when I can now better stand when clean and sober.

58 Younger, money sans baggage can augur trouble for a wandering eye.

59   She may not have been mine at the time, but I sure as heck wasn't going to share her…I had to cut bait.

60   It's the gazing that will get me.

61   The devil gets things close enough to right to be completely wrong.

62   I may not like the way a book or narrative ends, but it is not my decision.

63   For the wounded, even good memories are difficult.

64   Memories—even the good, liberated from the crypt—inflame seasonal scars peculiar to the blighted.

65   There are three comments I hold dear, even though they were likely stated with at least a hint of the pejorative: I'm the dog who wandered up to the right house; I'm a silver-tongued flatland Sherpa; and, I'm a redneck savant. Sadly, I can't even live up to those Southern ideals.

66   The only intellectual pursuit I enjoy as much as reading is having an intimate discussion with someone who listens interactively.

67   Every year sober, the holidays get easier to be entreated, but I still want them over before they begin.

68   My gut tells me stuff all the time.

69   Loving history while living in the present and avoiding the future is not easy for a compromised Luddite!

70   The Dirty South just is not going to ever conform to any box spuriously designed to mold it, us, or anything birthed, reared and likely smeared in this terraqueous soil.

71   It's not that I don't want to see what's right in front of me; I'm just not looking for it there.

72 To quote Scripture and not mean it is a shame.

73 Often, we blame others for creating division, when they simply unveil it.

74 I never was a "drunk," but I am an alcoholic.

75 If regional identity is pervasively assailed for the sake of perceived morality, then there will no longer be an identity to malign.

76 If the length of my hair, which brings me pleasure, disturbs someone, then he should be thankful for living a charmed life where unrelated minutiae is of great concern.

77 If the marginalized do not become empathetic as a result of their marginalization, then they will surely marginalize others, even while still being marginalized.

78 Being judgmental and gratuitously sharing unsolicited judgments—while often being right—does not make one a prophet.

79 For many, the Christmas season is green—my favorite color; for me, it is grey, yet the shade brightens yearly.

80 The only thing more beautiful than a gorgeous woman is a kind one who smiles often.

81 Church is not why we have Christmas; Christmas is why we have church.

82   It's not that I enjoy being cold when depressed, but short bursts of the frigid remind me I'm alive and painful memories are temporarily replaced.

83   When I try to please others, I am often miserable; when I don't try to please others, I'm often miserable: it's a wash, so be myself.

84   Turn-row philosophy matters.

85   Some folks are too busy being critical to realize they are being critical.

86   Most of what we lust after is not real and what is real is real dangerous.

87   I don't believe in haints, but I sure am afraid of 'em!

88   It's a strange feeling to be so thrilled that all your estranged children are safe and happy, yet to be so sad yourself.

Chapter 12

1. I am thankful to live in a time and place where I am free to reinvent myself regardless of recriminations.

2. Pedigree, hair, jewelry, club memberships, vocations, vacations, education, houses, cars, etc. are just skin on a manikin.

3. This may surprise some folks, but I don't want to be and look like everybody else, even if it greatly disturbs them and makes me look like a "fool!"

4. It really is nice when people you love don't get you a present for special occasions, because you don't have to tell them not to get you anything.

5. It's okay to be discouraged, but not okay to lose Faith, if our faith is in the right Person.

6. Smart folks, those with wisdom, recognize God.

7. The more we are thankful for less, the less we'll be dissatisfied with more.

8. Being tired sure makes me tired.

9. Those who con get conned, because that's all they know.

10. I'm interested in what interests me; I'm not interested in what doesn't interest me.

11. When Truth is no longer universally understood and definable, society and the individual are in real trouble.

12. I have all the time in the world to read, but I need more time.

13 The few friendships are all based on intellect, shared values, interactive listening, and gracious individualism.

14 Some of us survive by being flighty.

15 Only in the 21st-century First World could gender be relative.

16 How often am I thankful that my Eternal Salvation is based on Grace, while sadly sometimes thinking others is based on actions?

17 Everything will be revealed; we just don't get to dictate the timeline.

18 Roundman said gambling money has no home. Daddy was right.

19 Financial analyzing direly affects my philosophizing.

20 The grass is rarely greener, but sometimes different matters.

21 A rollin' stop still is not a stop.

22 It seems that successful people do a yeoman's job of putting mistakes in perspective.

23 I sure don't have a problem identifying someone else's resentments.

24 It's difficult to realize that there is a difference between good cigars and bad cigars until both have been smoked.

25 Human nature unchecked is foul by nature.

26 For all the current light of technology the world sure seems a darker place.

27 Loyalty should not trump morality; they work best hand-in-hand.

28 If money is involved and too important to those involved, then trust is suspect.

29 Organized religion has the potential to divide friends and family.

30 I often struggle with whether or not to go to Jerusalem over going to an organized church.

31 I am not so much a character, but I recognize, point out, and sure do appreciate characters.

32 The better I do, the better I want to do.

33 Transparency doesn't require constantly telling others something is transparent.

34 Over two and a half years clean and sober, I am still learning about my addiction.

35 I just thought, "Since I woke up early, I got my prayers out of the way!" Sad! Should be the best part of my day!

36 When others "ice me with silence" after I've been edgy, it's a good thing! Like icing a wound it mitigates inflammation, even though it's cold and doesn't feel good.

37 There are pros and cons to my being a hip shooter.

38 I have a defined palate, not necessarily a refined palate.

39 Sober, I no longer have an alcohol problem, but I'll always have a problem with alcohol.

40 You can't sneak up on a turtle.

41 I'm to the right of Attila the Hun politically and left of Matilda the Nun ecclesiastically.

42 I'm partial to my orifices being egresses and not ingresses.

43 I, too, tilt at windmills, and often appear as knight errant.

44 I like being different when I'm comfortable being different.

45 If God wanted to use an imperfect vessel, then leaving me around down here a little longer makes sense.

46 Cardinals—like Creation—can become so commonplace we often forget the miracle and the beauty!

47 Being a Young Turk has painful consequences, I know; I was one.

48 If I didn't do what I did before, then I might not be doing what I'm doing now.

49 I sure do feel better when I eat something, but not when I eat a lot of something.

50 My spouse gets lovelier as I begin to feel better about myself.

51 Character only seems to count if one doesn't support woke causes.

52 It is possible to worship someone, yet not honor her.

53 I consider taking a nap productive.

54 I've never seen anything swoop between traffic like a buzzard on some roadkill.

55 I can stop once I stop, but I can't stop once I start.

56 Every snake is not a moccasin, but every moccasin is a snake.

57 I don't want to pray and quote rote unless the rote helps make it real.

58 I want only intimate relationships, but they do take a lot out of me.

59 The fact I thought that tells me I think like that.

60 Subcutaneous sin is between the heart and the skin.

61 Sadly, I think I've spent most of my life trying to please myself by pleasing others.

62 If I am not myself then how can I ever find my self?

63 All I ever wanted to be when I grew up was an ectomorph…I just grew out.

64 Quick-witted can quickly lead to sin.

65 I feel guilty about feeling better about feeling guilty.

66 The only thing I don't feel guilty about is feeling guilty; unless it makes me guilty, then I feel guilty.

67 Capitalism is upside down when politicians, pastors, and bureaucratic elite "earn" more than business folks with skin in the game.

68 I can't handle too many highs and lows.

69 I can't drink alcohol sensibly.

70 I'm finally myself—whoever that is.

71 Grace is diminished when I don't accept God's forgiveness.

72 Some hairs just can't be straightened.

73 I don't want to know everything you know; I only want to know what you might know that I want to know.

74 You can't "quit for a while" if you're an alcoholic.

75 The glint, wink, and winsome nod of the golden elixir silently yet surreptitiously beckons quite surely to the conflicted addicted, camouflaging destruction and ultimately death.

76 If one consistently and with antipathy directs specious verisimilitudes toward those not in agreement, then apathy and avoidance will be the final answer.

77 I may at times be entertaining but I'm not here to entertain.

78 A desultory or cursory explanation regarding anything of import is never sufficient to alter another person's resolute preconceptions.

79 Don't bite the apple; it bites back.

80 It is surely one's prerogative to believe the Truth, or not; yet Truth is not dependent upon belief.

81 Loneliness alters behavior.

82 Belief in objective Truth is still subjective.

83 A controlling symbol can sure amp up an addict.

84 Unpleasant memories, nestled deep within the scarred—even on good days—are never more distant than a thin misty veil.

85 The wheels of bureaucracy have no tread and aren't really round

86 I am not trying' to emulate Maverick & Goose, but 'too tired' puts me too close to the danger zone.

87 Wealth, which is not inherently bad, usually always wins, even in church.

88 Too often, I so deeply desire supreme happiness for those I love that I blindly, yet willingly, overlook the obvious.

89 Saying "I can't help it" is not the same as admitting "I am helpless," which is the first step to recovery from anything.

13 Chapter

1. For many rapscallions—of whom I number as one—who speak of wanting to obey the law, we often find ourselves adhering to what we think we can get away with that's close to the law.

2. Everything that one does not agree with is not necessarily racial or bigoted, if it's in fact a fact.

3. Just because someone may be an alcoholic doesn't oblige another to say they are one.

4. The fine yet imperative line between the homophones "profit" and "prophet" is speedily waning.

5. I used to drive the Sativa Highway; now I soberly saunter the back roads on foot.

6. Don't be too hard on yourself—lonely sucks.

7. I'm only ever okay if my relationship with God is okay.

8. I hate being checked or corrected, but it's necessary.

9. The skinnier I get, the fatter I notice.

10. They don't call them masks for no reason.

11. I'm a philosopher who struggles with Philosophy.

12. Laurels are for wreaths, not for resting.

13. If it gets built, they may come, but if it's not maintained, they will leave.

14. Often slight inclines are not noticeable until you walk or bike them.

15   The hungrier I am, the sweeter the peach.

16   Junior Kimbrough and his simple style of Blues speak to the complex in me.

17   Past parenting regrets are never more distant than a sudden, paralyzing flashback.

18   Everyone is someone for whom Christ died.

19   Controllers change the definition when their lie is no longer believed.

20   I am so unworthy I don't fully recognize my unworthiness.

21   Memories of my past selfishness not only cause me great angst, but they also hold me accountable for my current selfishness.

22   "Southern philosopher" is likely just a euphemism for a redneck who occasionally does some conjecturing.

23   I never believed big corporations were Bobby Boucher's Mama's "the Devil," until they started mating with big government.

24   Black sheep are rarely constrained by societal norms.

25   Puppy love feels incredible, but often ends in a U-turn.

26   The failure of "true love" has no equal.

27   Just because one's path doesn't make sense does not mean it's the wrong one.

28   I knew Truth was in trouble several years ago when I saw an oft-repeated commercial with a cheesy, hot thang, validating the supposed salubrious pill as "real science." Real science has gone from redundant to oxymoronic.

29   For many, small talk is not just difficult…it is impossible.

30 As I age, I am not always successful in avoiding having opinions regarding things that do not concern me, but I am attempting to share them less frequently.

31 Kaleidoscopic thoughts while in a maelstrom are exhausting.

32 If global "peacekeeping" doesn't include a weapon, then consider it useless and one-sided.

33 Anything shy of a relationship with Jesus the Creator is too short or "nay enough."

34 Hegemony is.

35 All my dreams have water.

36 A big dog usually wins a pissing contest.

37 A pleasant wilderness is a safe place to be if Hope is in the One who placed you there.

38 The opaque, if investigated thoroughly, can lead to clearer vision.

39 I have difficulty retaining anything I'm not significantly interested in, except fluid.

40 Sadly, I can always eat.

41 Smokin'-hot, stranded-island love appears tasty, but is likely accompanied by a lot of "stank."

42 I'm rarely speechless when alone.

43 An expanded soul illuminates the pathway to a right spirit.

44 If folks in Recovery are serious about sobriety, then it is best for them to take their own vehicles when possible.

45   A little sweet, tastes mighty sweet, if you are not used to sweet.

46   I've got a Corona attention span with a Churchill appetite.

47   Most days, I just want to be on the water.

48   East is as far from West as Mercury is from Uranus.

49   My brilliance has no limits when alone...then, I get around people.

50   As a rule, I loathe bureaucracies and the tax dollars they rode in on.

51   The more I get to know myself, the more that is revealed.

52   For someone living in the present, I sure have a lot to learn about being "present."

53   The membrane between being a "drunk" and an "alcoholic" is thinner than most folks recognize.

54   I'm out there; they're out there; we just are not necessarily in the same place out there, wherever out there is.

55   The best way to not need a weapon is to carry one.

56   Get to know thy neighbor; when the revolution comes, it might come in handy.

57   Arguing with a closed door is fruitless.

58   The tightest circle includes resentment, hatred and victimization—non-stop circular.

59   How easy it is to follow the devil in disguise down into the belly of his lair.

60   Some holes never fill nor heal; often, the best we can hope for is a thin, semi-permeable covering.

61 If living "right," staying hydrated, eating healthy, and diligently beseeching God's protection is not enough, then I reckon it will be time to meet Him face-to-face; and, that's a good thing; no, the best of things.

62 I never agreed with folks who broke the law yet hated the system for checking them; now, as I've aged, I understand folks who obey the law, yet still fear it.

63 For the active addict, gambling makes every endeavor more "interesting." For the recovering addict, it leads to a pit of despair where joy goes to die.

64 A fool and his money have no trouble attracting honey.

65 My buddy, Carb, always said money is nuthin' but units.

66 Money can buy amenities, pleasure and comfort, but is essentially worthless in the pursuit of true Peace and Joy.

67 I may have fallen off the proverbial watermelon cart, but I didn't completely bust my melon.

68 If I consistently over time, consistently admit I've always been a fool, then it might indicate I'm likely still a fool in the present.

69 I know less than I know.

70 To deny oneself the very thing one loves to please the One one loves, is not always easy, but it's right.

71 As an alcoholic and big-eater, I find it's not always easy to experience pleasure and relief outside the knowns of alcohol and food; yet it's possible, and eminently worth it.

72 Behind many an atheist's facade lies a belief in the otherworldly.

73 It is nigh on impossible to discern a smiling face behind a mask.

74 You don't have to teach a male dog to hump.

75 The older I get, the smarter I am about my stupidity.

76 I can make fun of my intelligence; you can't.

77 The only sound competing with silence, peace-wise, is water cascading down rocks and the dinner bell.

78 I often feel like a time-traveling pilgrim with a sense and love of time and place.

79 To make peace with Murphy's inevitable law it behooves me to extenuate expectations, live in the present, and to trust God in all things.

80 Even contrarians serve a purpose.

81 Everyone has insecurities; some can deal with and hide them better than others.

82 Everything referred to as cheap is relative, as is everyone thought to be rich or poor.

83 'Tis no greater gift for an imperfect father than to receive a daughter's forgiveness.

84 Hard memories become easier to be entreated as I soften.

85 Garnering rights is a right in a society predicated on rights; preferential treatment is not.

86 When a man is "The Man," it is hard to trust The Man who is just a man.

87 Thin, spider-web strands of brilliance are easily severed by a lot of self-induced stupid.

88 Strutters who hate on strutters are still just struttin'.

89 It may be hard to determine when buttermilk starts going bad, but it is not hard to know when it is bad.

90 To truly learn a lesson, one has to live to learn it.

91 The only reason I don't whistle Dixie is I can't whistle.

Chapter 14

1. For alcoholics, time sober is not irrelevant, but every alcoholic is just as sober today as the person who just got sober today.

2. On rainy Delta fall days, a stogie, a good read and some thick contemplation can help ease pre-seasonal affectation.

3. A sad thing about being right is those who are proven wrong will rarely admit it.

4. There exist a deep, wide crevice between owning a person and being responsible for someone.

5. Fall, as a season, evokes a kaleidoscope of memories: the good, the bad, and the downright ugly.

6. It's imperative that humanity stand up and defend righteousness, but not do so self-righteously.

7. Blanket judgment of absentee Dads may be an easy call, but that doesn't make it right, just ill-informed.

8. To control the uncontrollable is no control at all.

9. When in the woods, one is not out of the woods until one is out of the woods; when in the water, one is not out of the water until one is out of the water.

10. There often seems to be a disconcerting relationship between privilege and ungratefulness.

11. I am not trying to be something I am not; I am whatever I am, whatever that happens to be.

12. A carpet baggin' scalawag is someone born here, moved away, then comes back to begin the fleecing and the know-it-alls.

13. I didn't like it; so, I ate it all.

14. Silent soliloquies are rarely silent.

15. If it were easy to understand, I likely wouldn't ruminate on it, whatever it is.

16. When contacting governmental agencies regarding a dire situation, my expected and rarely disappointed disappointing response from them: "Continue to hold, an agent will be with you shortly!"

17. I appreciate quick-witted people; dim-witted-quick-witted people frustrate.

18. Occam's Razor likely confirms that no answer often suffices as the best answer.

19. I wish it were not so, but I discourage easily.

20. I went from smokin' to tokin' to herfin'—may seem linear but it is not.

21. I enjoy sharing things I wrote or recorded spontaneously while alone.

22. It's futile to hate on someone's "perfect life"—'cause it is not.

23. In a totalitarian form of authoritarian government, egregious, liberty-robbing fiat is instantaneous; in a devolving democracy, the process is slower, yet just as sure.

24. Evil seeks to pervert and bend the Truth to justify its corruption. It needs Truth's approval to beguile the witless as well as the clever.

25. A Delta Brahmin is no Brahmin at all.

26 Getting back on track doesn't mean starting with a marathon.

27 Being "intellectually aloof" doesn't inherently make one intellectual or aloof.

28 God is the author of instinct.

29 When frustrated, foolishness pours out of my mouth like snowmelt on a hot day in the Himalayas.

30 I pray God will help me try not to act like I'm more than I am or less than I am, but I will be a thoughtful who I am.

31 It sure is hard to be humble when I have no reason not to be humble.

32 Abstinence with booze and drugs, moderation with food, and circumspection with exercise is not bulletproof but it sure helps an older addict like me.

33 I enjoy the company of strong people with a moral compass; I do not enjoy the company of headstrong folks regardless of the compass.

34 I am thankful for a spouse who allows me to be totally vulnerable, and then, assiduously protects that vulnerability.

35 Dogs go where they are fed.

36 I want to be the turtle that doesn't follow the bale of his podnas off the log.

37 I've been fooled by religion, not by God.

38 Everybody feels sorrow.

39 If I looked to God as constantly and with verve the same way my dog Dandy looks at me, to ascertain my next move, God would be thrilled with my devotion.

40   I am often careless with carelessness.

41   There are times when unexpectedly I truly realize how many people I have hurt, let down, and used over a lifetime of selfishness.

42   Money is worrisome, that is partly why I am bereft of dough.

43   Working clean and hard to feel high makes life easier and more enjoyable than getting high easily which makes life hard and much less enjoyable.

44   Privilege is not relegated or specific to the wealthy.

45   Temporal is not eternal, though eternity includes the temporal.

46   Just when I think I understand Grace, I receive more and realize I know nothing.

47   In error, I presumed artificial intelligence an oxymoron.

48   It is likely not an "amend" if I tell them why I've having to make an amend.

49   I desire bold humility and humble boldness.

50   I sure can't control the actions of others if I have trouble controlling mine.

51   I don't like to contemplate death, but thoughts on the brevity of life are unavoidable.

52   It is perfectly acceptable for one to be thankful a philanthropic program exists, yet not feel compunction to support it.

53   As Christians, too many of us hedge our bets.

54   My psyche is more fragile than I care to admit. Only God.

55 Strange may be exciting but it can be destructive.

56 I am envious of my friends, who, like the butterfly, can draw nourishment from feces. They find the good and enjoyable in situations where I seemingly extract so little value.

57 My addict brain is like a West African trickster.

58 Beware smooth lies from inside thy own cranium.

59 Be a friend; make an amend.

60 Is it Society's fault? Yes and No!

61 Saw a picture of Rome; thought of Dino Martin; immediately craved a glass of red wine! Sobriety is not easy even three years down the road for a recovering alcoholic/addict! Only God!

62 John Barleycorn is not a problem, unless he is; then, he's a big problem.

63 To honor one for an inherited trait is not equivalent to a celebration of one's achievements.

64 To assume a male with long hair is liberal politically is as bold as assuming a short-haired male is politically conservative.

65 "De repente" in Spanish means suddenly! Coincidence? I think not.

66 The proverbial rising boulder can only be understood via Scripture.

67 How quickly Gain of Function segues to Loss of Function.

68 Duality does not necessarily imply cognitive dissonance.

69 Trash in the Mississippi Delta is sadly like cicadas—white noise to the familiar.

70   Often, my procrastination is a result of my overthinking where to put something instead of just putting something somewhere.

71   There is no Biblical evidence for golf in Heaven.

72   As a Christian, my pursuit of coolness hinders and conflicts with my need for righteousness.

73   Social Media has convinced me that I was never intended to know the innermost thoughts of stranger and friend.

74   A honed conscience still sloughs off much guilt. It has to.

75   I have terrible social anxiety; I combat it by trying to be social.

76   We don't end up in Recovery because everything is okay.

77   To inflame is not a good thing, but, if necessary, make it for a good cause—prepare for searing blowback.

78   You do you; I'll do me; and we'll just see.

79   For the life of me, I cannot comprehend how the modern, professing Christian can think it is okay to terminate the life of a miraculous child—fearfully and wonderfully created by the God they serve—while still in the mother's womb. However, there is absolutely forgiveness.

80   If one belongs to enough subcultures, it still does not give one entree to the dominant culture.

81   Malachi doesn't enjoy bathroom humor.

82   Before responding to another's statements, it behooves one to cogitate on words like: seems, in my opinion, assume, some, few, one, many, likely, possible, could be, in some instances, and whether they are capitalized or not...

83   An olive branch extended is best served with olives attached.

84   I need to be outside.

85   Faust may be mythical, but Faustian deals are not.

86   Discerning good and evil can sometimes be akin to distinguishing between cilantro and Italian parsley, they look similar until you sniff and chew.

87   I'm never further than a click away from going to ground…for good.

Chapter 15

1. Prickly pears have few friends.

2. Two years seemed like a lifetime that first frightening night of Army Basic Training 40 years ago; just as that first night of four weeks spent in addiction treatment three years ago. Time is relative, if it's relevant.

3. I love Jeremiah Johnson, but most days I want to watch him not be him.

4. I beat my own drum, poorly, but I still don't want advice from an unsolicited percussionist.

5. For someone who claims to be bothered because he doesn't fit in, I sure seem not to want to fit in.

6. Bully a peace-loving Southerner long enough and one will get a reaction; nobody wins in the end, conflict unavoidable.

7. The mere mention of the word Bourbon still makes me lick my over-three-years-sober lips.

8. Remo ergo sum a bum.

9. Fear is an ugly thing.

10. If nothing from nothing leaves nothing, and I started naked with nothing, then I've lost nothing and will leave naked with nothing... except God's good Grace—now, that's Something.

11. To lightly monetize a passion does make some sense to me.

12. At times, I realize I'm not claustrophobic when I normally would be; then, I become claustrophobic when I shouldn't be.

13 The contrived pastoral cadence of many "pulpiteers" is difficult to be entreated by those accustomed to succinct, plain speech.

14 Progressivism is often parasitic, not symbiotic, and is fundamentally juxtaposed against a traditional, classical, orthodox understanding of Judeo-Christianity.

15 Sadly, too often in America, the most church-going folks are the least thankful.

16 Life really is a bit of a lethal mind game.

17 Governmental coercion is always suspicious.

18 Jesus wore my cross.

19 The longer I live the better I understand Jimmy Vickers living under a bridge.

20 I'm guilty of original sin, but it isn't due to my inherited skin color; it's due to my fallen nature confirmed by my actions.

21 It is not easy corralling a Montroy.

22 True Faith is not ephemeral.

23 I fear my sensibilities often override my sense, leaving me with the fraying vicissitudes of the visceral.

24 As an addict and an alcoholic, I find comfort, hope and help in the recognition of both.

25 The amalgamation of distinct personalities is usually where the persona is found.

26 Rivers connect the contiguous like synapses connect the disparate.

27 I am lighter on the water than in it or out of it.

28   I best experience the elements on the water.

29   Water facilitates contemplation as it does transportation, one drop at a time.

30   Inertia can be complicated.

31   Seeking strange water is not like seeking "strange," it's best to stick with your woman, but new water can be sweet!

32   Every single time someone hates on me because of my shared or not shared worldview, he or she reinforces my beliefs.

33   Sadly, as a Christian, I spent most of my life emphasizing works over Grace, while still not doing the works.

34   I am not much of a toe-tester when two feet will do.

35   One can't reeducate right!

36   I am not trying too hard to walk like anybody else.

37   I am a product of my past, even the parts neither others nor I understand.

38   Faust doesn't get a redo.

39   As a recovering addict, I still find myself jonesing for jonesing.

40   I don't enjoy watching ultimate fighting on TV, but if one ever sees an ultimate fighter without cauliflower ears, then they either are "that good" or they haven't been fighting long.

41   Anything I might accomplish this late in life will not change anybody's life, but if I can make a few folks—myself included—"think," then I'll call it worthwhile.

42 I may hate abortion, but I do not hate those who have had one, neither does God; in fact, He Loves them dearly.

43 When frustrating things happen to me or to those I love, I am quick to chalk it up to God's protecting us from something. Should I also not see God's will in all things and thank him constantly in the mundane and difficult?

44 I ran out of throwing-stones a long time ago; sadly, I still try to chunk one now and again.

45 Ironically, I break more egg yolks being gentle than deliberate.

46 Too many variables and, conversely, too many constants, can exhaust the attention-deficit.

47 If I appear to pen something not layered with multiple, often esoteric entendres, then I likely didn't write it.

48 I don't like pressure points.

49 I may no longer drink and use drugs, but I am undeniably still an addict.

50 Money burns a hole in my pocket even when I don't have any.

51 Pretty doesn't mean one is smart any more than pretty means one is not smart. Pretty and smart are not necessarily similar or antithetical.

52 Too much grind can take an addict down before quick.

53 I cannot deny that I must deny that which is difficult to deny.

54 In retrospect, I often look back and say, "I was hanging on to sanity by a thread." In reality, sanity was kaput; I was hanging on to life by a thread!

55 When in active addiction, I was not ashamed of the substances I used, so in Recovery I am not going to be ashamed that I don't use.

56 I would like to say, "How in the hell did I get to be as old as I am;" but hell had nothing to do with it—quite the opposite.

57 Four-letter words may be an earful, but it's the two-letter words in Spanish that are killing me.

58 Just because I was "actin' a fool," doesn't mean everything I did was foolish.

59 Southern philosophers understand the dire need for a rest day after a rest day full of beaucoup thinking.

60 I don't listen to many folks, but I do listen to my wife, not because I have to, but because I want to and need to.

61 Sadly, often too often, the biggest part of life is the least important.

62 If my tombstone epitaph reads, "He died without too much crap in his neck," then I'll consider it a life well lived.

63 Metal on metal makes my fillings squeal and my equilibrium reel.

64 It don't bother me if folks don't be using the King's English as long as they know better or don't know better.

65 I am as sure that I've had Covid without being tested as others likely are having been tested.

66 When the Feds finally figure out they can't solve or fix anything, then they advocate for states' rights.

67 I never cease to be amazed at the sheer number of ultra-gifted folks who are ultra-stupid, and the plethora of famous people who are ultra-ultra-stupid.

68 Other than the loss of a child, there is little heartbreak worse than the heartbreak for a heartbroken or broken child! Only God!

69 Addicts know addicts; you really can't fool a conman or conwoman for long.

70 When comedians apologize for not being politically correct, they might have lost their relevance and mojo, and surely have lost their edge—for good or ill.

71 I never could walk a tightrope, particularly when high-strung.

72 The Master and the world's puppet master are not the same entity—quite the antithesis.

73 I am not a fan of sending kids off to school if it makes them "smarter," yet less spiritual.

74 Expediency for expediency's sake can lead to a fissured bridge ready to torpedo the most honest pilgrim.

75 Thoughts of prior mania exhaust me without the mania.

76 Smart people want to be recognized for being smart; beautiful people want to be recognized for being beautiful; powerful people want to be recognized for being powerful; narcissists want to be recognized for never being wrong; and, humble people don't want to be recognized at all.

77 When duality includes venality, an unhealthy paradox lies within.

78 Faith is just that.

79 Mania is a "drug," just ask a recovering addict what the withdrawal is like; the ensuing depression does get better, it just takes a while.

80 At times "nothing" can wear me out.

81 Being referred to as sheep can be a positive thing or a negative thing.

82 "Yellow dog" anything is dangerous; Truth should trump loyalty, yet it rarely does.

83 I may have been a Boy Scout, but I wasn't a Boy Scout.

84 Every day that I am not in the Big House is a good day.

85 A critic who offers a critique should not be summarily equated with a quibbling faultfinder who excels at criticism.

86 Being a critic is not necessarily the same as being one who criticizes; conversely, one who criticizes is not necessarily deigned a critic.

87 The ephemeral, non-corporeal nature of spirituality is complex.

88 Discursive descents often lead to Truth reflected.

89 I spent a lot of years high and ready to die.

90 Working a briar patch makes a good farmer, but sandy land doesn't hurt.

91 I pray God will always help my Faith to be implied, even when timidity sets in, and circumspect words fail me.

Chapter 16

1. I'd rather live in a tent in the Mississippi Delta than a penthouse in New York City.

2. I sure have often been easily duped for someone who thinks he is not easily duped.

3. Only God can shoulder the world's hurt.

4. Folks cannot comply their way out of tyranny to freedom.

5. I may at times saddle my high horse, but I sure have no business riding it.

6. If theories proven can lead to fact, then a conspiracy theory should not be considered a pejorative when it leads to truth.

7. If someone or some entity forces others to go to "Jerusalem," it likely is not a mandate from God.

8. I miss the simplicity of the 1970s.

9. For an addict, a night of a 1,000 sips is not a slip.

10. Victorian sensibilities may be rigid, but that doesn't mean they are all wrong.

11. First impressions should never have the final say, but they are informative.

12. I live my Recovery from addiction out loud, because, anything I hide becomes a problem.

13. I eventually, albeit too slowly, realize my heart is not right when I get to judging others for my sins.

14 "A fool and his money may soon be parted"; sadly, a fool and his politics rarely are.

15 Sunshine matters.

16 I have an easier time staying "present" in silence sans stimuli.

17 Tilting at windmills may be futile, yet I still tilt.

18 Turn profound into an adverb and it can easily precede stupid.

19 Ladder climbing is a compelling yet dangerous business.

20 Those who soldier still need a foxhole at times; otherwise, overexposure can be a killer.

21 Until the scales are leveled, the Republic is surely lost.

22 The horror of divorce is superseded only by the abuse and death of a child.

23 I've known lonely, intimately; I didn't handle it well.

24 Sometimes walking through the past can appear as painful as the past.

25 I hurt so badly I couldn't get up; I hurt so badly I had to get up.

26 In this age of faux and shortages, I wonder if Count Dracula sucks beet juice.

27 You know you're tired when you don't want to get up outta the tub even when lukewarm has sailed.

28 I have trouble regulating.

29 It's difficult chasing butterflies when they've all blown away.

30 Hot water stirred is a heck of a lot hotter than hot water still.

31 I gravitate toward alienation in life, music, literature and thought—though it is tinder for depression—it doesn't overstimulate; negative space provides breathing room, the freedom to find one's way to safety and beauty.

32 To trivialize the Poet is to deprecate humanity.

33 Pornography is a malignant gateway drug enslaving both the perpetrator and the victim.

34 Memories aren't reality until they are.

35 The vanity of life is the thinking person's nightmare.

36 When I pontificate aloud, sadly, I avoid more than I address.

37 If I have to tell folks who know how sensitive I am that I'm feeling "hard," I probably am not! Hard is not a feeling.

38 If there is a thin membrane between politics and money, it is imperceptible.

39 Duality: I think a drink will make things better; I know a drink will make things worse.

40 Even on the best of days, after too many days, it's just another day where I'm holding on to Eternity.

41 The heart speaks clearly when shattered.

42 On the days when pain outweighs pleasure, the Hope and certainty of Eternity make the weight worthwhile.

43 There is Wisdom in brevity.

44 Symbiosis is beautiful in theory.

45 True evil can only be rectified with and by a reckoning with God Almighty.

46 Stress is this addict's hair-trigger.

47 The known darkness of the rabbit-hole of resentment still tempts.

48 Romantic and commercially romantic are not necessarily the same thing.

49 Only reason I don't talk more crap is because my skin is thin.

50 Yakkin' is a double entendre.

51 Caring for my sobriety is more than just staying sober.

52 I used to confuse mania with just having energy.

53 I intimately understand the feeling of being alone in a crowded room.

54 I struggle with regulating, yet I must.

55 Eyes fascinate me. They tell the old, old story and give sight to insight.

56 When I am tempted, often, to be ungrateful, I am reminded there are hundreds of millions of people who would love to have my life—warts and all.

57 Three and a half years clean and sober and I still miss the warmth and burn of very cold bourbon.

58 Anything more complex than simple hurts my simply complicated head.

59 Snoop is Dope is a multiple entendre.

60   Being normal is an unattainable desire.

61   Few truly recognize a diamond when they see one, but those who do, have the pleasure of mining an inestimable treasure—for my Loves!

62   Just when I think our nation has hit a new low, the sun comes up and…BOOM!

63   Multiple entendres can't be explained in a sound bite, nor will I try.

64   "Most thought is backed by a reason" is not the equivalent of "most thought is backed by reason"; yet both can still be unreasonable.

65   An exhilarating novel with sagacious discourse—uttered or internalized—always results in my reaching bedside for a pen to mark well-constructed, thoughtful sentences expressed by a fictional character.

66   Evidence of intelligence is not indicative of common sense.

67   A child's behavior—cognizant or not—toward an adult is often a mirror reflection of how a parent views the same person.

68   When sorely tempted, I pray God will help me be who I should be and not necessarily who I want to be.

69   In a progressive tense and sense, I am writing a book that does not end until I do…

70   A wife's respect fuels a desire in a man to be worthy of that respect.

71   Customers are only right when they are right—otherwise, they are wrong.

72   It is frightening how easy it is in our instant-gratification, social-media world not only to disparage someone or some entity, but to do it assuming another's identity.

73 We are not made more human by communicating with other humans through bytes and bits.

74 Stress amplifies fragility.

75 Sadly, I am affected by more opinions than I respect.

76 Doubling down on stupid makes one "stupider."

77 If there is to be a "Come to Jesus" meeting, it is likely more productive if those involved come to Jesus first.

78 Sometimes a mountain of crap is bigger than one man's shovel!

79 Mass mainstream media makes most masticate not on ideas but on perceived wrongs.

80 Most of us are not only emotionally stunted by divorce, we revert to times long, long ago.

81 There are no forearm shivers in baseball.

82 Sometimes I'm scared of just about everything; at other times I'm scared of nothing except irritating Mr. Chuck Norris.

83 If the devil says to fly, it's best to walk.

84 If people feel threatened by us and we know we are to love them, then we should encourage them, not resent them—easier said than done.

85 I may be tone deaf, but beautiful classical music, particularly a mellow cello, reminds me that God will one day wipe away all my tears, fears, and bad memories.

86   Internationally, I have no clue what is really going on; we are not being told the Truth, but I do at least have a clue that I have no clue, and that keeps me hopeful.

87   An extreme diet is nothing but a "dry drunk."

Chapter 17

1. "Win one for the Gipper" is a great sporting-event battle cry, but I'm growing weary of the talking heads using it as a justification for America entering another life-taking, finance draining, elite-only-gaining costly worldwide conflict in a region few Americans historically understand, can spell, or even know where it is.

2. The "whole package" rarely recognizes a need for God.

3. I want to be recognized as excellent in Wisdom, above average in looks and normal in size—the recognition of none of these is important.

4. When doves cry for war, it is time for Peace!

5. Peer reviews in scientific journals are imperative and ensure validity; in Congress, quite the antithesis.

6. We are inclined to love certain people for the same reason we love dogs—they are faithful.

7. At my age and mental wherewithal, if I don't leave a familiar item in the exact location where I left it last time, then it should be considered lost.

8. In many countries the media is suppressed; in America the press is often the oppressor.

9. Humility wins the long day.

10. Peace in the world first blooms in the individual heart.

11. Sadly, daily, it's becoming easier not to trust our own country's motives and actions as we increasingly question the motives and actions of other countries.

12   There is no solace in the Darkness.

13   I feel guilty about envying people who don't feel guilty.

14   It is not always easy being easy, nor easy being not easy—there is no easy.

15   We have not even begun to see the beginning of woes.

16   I'll never be close to all right until this reckoning addict treats food like I now do whiskey and weed.

17   A thin thread of brilliance does not nullify a #2 washtub full of stupid; and conversely, a #2 washtub heavy laden with brilliance does not always nullify even a thin thread of sheer stupidity.

18   If Pogo is correct and "the enemy is us," then it sure makes it hard at times to recognize the enemy.

19   In my case, nuthin' from nuthin' leaves nuthin' and I need something.

20   Too much work is inherently deleterious to my ardent philosophizing.

21   Sometimes, it's almost as much fun inflating a grand ego as it is deflating it.

22   Along with white noise, silence is the best sound around.

23   Stagflation is an imminent conflagration.

24   Some folks are funny…one time, but I can only stand so much clowning.

25   Ad hominem attacks are a continual reminder that mankind remains largely unredeemed.

26 Screwtape is among us.

27 Addicts love dogs because we can always trust them better than we can trust ourselves.

28 When 80% of a population thinks something is right, it just might be wrong.

29 As a somewhat stunted Christian, my Faith will not grow if I continue to keep a "list" of those I resent.

30 Bringing every American soldier home alive has segued from a reality to nothing more than a slogan.

31 I'm an easy con until I'm not; I'm a hard con until I'm not.

32 Celebrating base sub-groups and unhealthy elements of a culture likely contributes to present-day malaise.

33 I'll never be him and he'll never be me; I'm okay with that, hopefully he is.

34 Starts and restarts matter.

35 Periodically, it does concern me that it doesn't concern me that I am not more concerned in my belief that our government wants many of us dead.

36 Chevy Chase was wrong when he said, "Francisco Franco is not dead"; the protean Franco changed skins and walks among us in the form of governmental, mainstream and social media.

37 Feckless does as feckless is.

38 Most of the time, the best thing I can do is not have an opinion.

39 A manufactured crisis is still a crisis.

40   It's never too late, yet never is too late.

41   I was never at Peace in addictive addiction.

42   Kayaking reinforces my deep-seated belief that life—like water—is inseparably fluid.

43   Many sayings should be catalysts for thought, not for public comment.

44   I want to do things differently from others, not to be different, but because I am different.

45   Good Manners matter, yet they do not magically manifest.

46   My wife understands my limitations; what a blessing!

47   A few days in the wilderness inform and remind a fella of his strengths and weaknesses.

48   I don't need to make a decision about tomorrow based on the end of a tough day today.

49   True class is not evidenced by how much money people have or by the finery they wear but by how they treat others.

50   I should never base the coming day on how I feel when I wake up in the morning.

51   I'm a good guy only when compared to really bad guys, which is a poor measuring stick.

52   I love the Mississippi Delta, where a person can see forever, or at least far enough.

53   When I often think someone else is the elephant in the room, I really should be more introspective.

54 Splitting theological hairs is a first-world luxury.

55 Today, everything is suspect: to question is not antithetical to trust, to inquire does not make one a cynic.

56 Every high horse I get to ridin' simply precedes a great fall.

57 Every slope is not slippery, but the ones that are, are.

58 There are those likely as flawed as I, but they trump it with confidence.

59 I truly believe God lets me see more wildlife now that my finger is no longer on the trigger.

60 I continue to be amazed at the elites in their 60s, 70s and 80s who lie, cheat, steal and horde large sums of money; it is not going to spend in the soon-to-be afterlife—it might work more like demerits.

61 Folks who believe PTSD is relegated only to wartime terror might want to consider the effect an ugly divorce with children in the cross hairs has on all involved.

62 Modernity—laden with amenities—still has its challenges.

63 If we allow our ideology or theology to trump Truth, then shame on us.

64 I have firmly believed for a while that the sexual abuse of children coupled with human trafficking is rampant worldwide and the blackmailing of the culprits in high places on both sides of any ideological aisle is the foul evidence that the kingdom of darkness is at the helm. Only God!

65 One of the few times my foolish optimism outweighs my debilitating pessimism is when I avoid the doctor when I probably shouldn't.

66 Calumny doesn't become me.

67   I can't control the past or the future, and my limited control of the present is fraught with naught; yet I persist.

68   Indifference can be as odious as hatred.

69   Thinking about the marvels of memory fascinates me when I can remember to think about it.

70   If one would not want a history professor teaching Physics, then please don't require me to customize something outside my established niche.

71   My earliest memory was sensitive.

72   Too much stimulation and music make me want to drink and get high; one song will do!

73   God, others and I like me better clean & sober; so, it's worth the trouble to stay so.

74   If we experience life fully in the present progressive tense, the imperfect won't eat us alive.

75   Too often we want what we shouldn't, can't have, and wouldn't want if we get it.

76   A desire for "strange" is the enemy of gratefulness.

77   The under-appreciated blackbird in the midst of a sea of male cardinals should be considered magnificent.

78   America has been groomed and grooming for a long time.

79   When I hear, "an expert said," without attribution, I usually believe it is "suspect."

80   The "thought life" of even a "good" man is a constant struggle with today's image inundation.

81 Inauthentic images disturb me.

82 No matter how we inadvertently screw up our kids their resilience with God's help is astounding.

83 If I would learn to always be kind, then I could avoid apologizing when I'm unkind, even if right.

84 It's hard to not require perfection from those who act as if they are, but we still shouldn't.

85 Some folks may be right, but they are still difficult to listen to for a myriad of reasons.

86 "Did you like that sermon " is interrogative. "Didn't you like that sermon!" is rhetorical.

87 My body is always waiting for me to eat out again, so it can swell disproportionately.

88 I am not proud of it, and it does have dire consequences, however, I will cut my nose off to spite my face.

89 Everything affects me.

Chapter 18

1. One proof, for me, that God exists is in the paradox of creation's continuity and individuality.

2. I don't write for others; I write for me. I just happen to share it often.

3. Even when praised, many artists still feel misunderstood.

4. Small talk becomes more difficult the longer I am sober.

5. Saying one is committed doesn't mean one is committed.

6. Plans for the unexpected still precede the unexpected.

7. Those who find "religion" usually move up the ecclesiastical pecking order quickly if they have money.

8. Gilded the lily may be, yet still difficult to kill.

9. If one lives long enough, loneliness is not just a possibility but a certainty.

10. I write like I think and think like I write.

11. Regarding righteousness, I am as fallen as a Confederate statue in downtown Seattle.

12. Sadly, we too often don't hear God until we have to. He is not silent; we just don't listen until we feel some need.

13. Mania does not become me.

14. Death in the Delta gets around quickly.

15. Death up-close causes me to revisit my beliefs regarding Eternal life.

16   I used to be high, drunk and happy until I was high, drunk and unhappy; now, I'm clean sober and happy.

17   Bureaucracies and government don't hire the hungry.

18   I am blessed not for being a good and faithful servant; I am blessed due to a good and faithful God.

19   The closer I get to Eternity the more I contemplate Eternity.

20   If we question whether we were close friends, it is a question worth asking.

21   Most resentments last long past their due date.

22   Being a victim keeps one a victim.

23   When it comes to dealing with "The Man," we get what we allow.

24   Pygmalion pursuits are usually done more for the "orchestrator" than the beneficiary.

25   Being "on" takes a lot out of an introvert.

26   Protean protagonists may irritate our entrenched affectations and sensibilities, yet they are more authentic than the fictionally stagnant.

27   Things we take for granted soon disappear.

28   By nature, the individual is the center of the universe; by intention, he or she is not.

29   The Federal teat promises nourishment to the willing, yet is void of sustainable sustenance while enslaving the addicted and inoculating nothing.

30   Kinda ridiculous for "The Facebook" to get political because it's segued into mostly us old folks sharing grand-baby pics.

31   To fear the unknown is futile, as it is unknown.

32   Sadly, for America to right herself, all of us are going to have to feel a lot of pain until those with a higher pain tolerance and harder heads sustain more than enough distress.

33   I only notice what I notice.

34   The complexities, duality and Faulkneresque affectations rooted in the agrarian Deep South fascinate many; though, they will remain unknown, reviled, and misunderstood by the provincially non-provincial.

35   The Deep South is the elephant's graveyard for a Southerner.

36   I don't argue with the ignorant, haters, trolls, nor pot stirrers––at least I shouldn't.

37   Everything has a source, except God; He is the God of sources.

38   High meadows give me sight and Hope.

39   Too many cages are self-made; the key is on the inside.

40   One can be kaleidoscopic, yet still on the spectrum.

41   One may be on the spectrum because of the kaleidoscopic.

42   We may see the same thing, but our lenses are not the same.

43   I will not judge or condemn a man for one handshake, but I will keep both eyes open.

44   "We are the world" as a mantra/song may become true once we stop being "the world."

45 For someone always seeking balance, I sure do create a mighty lot of imbalance.

46 I do a lot of thinking while chair sitting, but I don't get my thinking out of my head until I walk, pray or paddle.

47 It's best not to hug a Blue Blood unless they make the first move.

48 Sorry, I can't make it; I'm old and sober.

49 My past still has the power to crush me, if I let it.

50 I rarely get full. I see the problem.

51 Tribes are emboldened when the divisive divide.

52 Though I share original quotes as sound bites, they are not intended for sound-bite comments—they deserve deeper, Socratic reflection and discussion of the multiple entendres.

53 I should learn to be hungry before I have to learn to be hungry.

54 People who really are "making a difference" don't need to say they are makes a difference.

55 Doing "something" does not necessarily equate to doing something effectively.

56 If I could make some peace with being a lil' hungry, like I have with being bourbon-thirsty, I might just be alright—one day at a time.

57 Be careful when praying for a hot babe who prays; one just might get a hot babe who preys.

58 I prefer to not be integrally tied to a society where all three measures of socio-economic central tendency—mean, median and mode—are exactly the same.

59 I sometimes worry about not having a retirement plan, but if I had one, I would worry about my retirement plan.

60 Wildlife is life.

61 The Elite are not governed by the same set of rules, expectations and mores they legislate, require, and demand of the rest of us. Why? They don't have to answer that.

62 I'm a capricious chameleon: I can be who I think you want me to be until I want to be who I want to be.

63 Programs help, but the participants make all the difference.

64 I may not be an anti-social drinker, nor am I an anti social-drinker, but I am not a social drinker either.

65 I dig the laid-back lifestyle, but for those in the service industry, it will not kill 'em to have a sense of urgency.

66 Anytime I do something, I then have to not do something.

67 Because I am a sensitive marshmallow (according to my siblings), I have to act all hard so folks won't figure out I'm a marshmallow, because then I am going to be a non-marshmallow and get all hard.

68 The only way I have found to get comfortable with white-capping waves is to spend a lot of time being uncomfortable with white-capping waves.

69 The Irish blessing stating, "…may the wind always be at your back…" takes on a whole new level of significance for a paddler.

70 There are plenty of ways I might end up dying, but exhaustion is not likely one of 'em.

71 There is a definable construct difference between a safe space and a safe place.

72 Once one is aware of alienation, it's hard to avoid it.

73 Everybody is marginalized somewhere.

74 Some folks are like baklava, super-saccharine-sweet, pleasant to meet, but one can only handle so much and only on special occasions.

75 I never cease to be amazed at the number of gifted folks who cross my path and later do something extraordinary in a different discipline or arena than I imagined.

76 The ethereal "high road" is subjective when it comes to resisting evil.

77 Condescension is the apex of arrogance.

78 Tribes always have been, always will be, and will always be antithetical to one-world, faux solidarity.

79 Homogenizing tribes doesn't work, better to encourage tribe members to love God and others, which will engender harmony while avoiding hegemony.

80 Some folks can never turn the finger around.

81 It's one thing to deal with and be familiar with alienation; it's another to court it.

82 There is no known schematic for the addict, yet there are distinct wiring commonalities.

83 I've been a bit lonely all my life, though not always alone; conversely, though often alone, I'm not always lonely.

84 We who have been given so much just throw it away.

85 There is a big difference between "I'm going to start…," and, "I have started…"

86 Intellectually bright does not necessarily equate to commonsensical.

87 I'm glad those who knew what was "best for me" didn't get to chart my path; though I may have avoided a lot of pitfalls—dug by my own hand—I never would have learned to crawl out of the mire, a necessary skill for a bruised cat like me.

88 One thing lower than an elite's perception of those beneath him is the elite himself.

Chapter 19

1. I don't do crowds.

2. There is a distinct gulf between a Christian nation, and a nation founded on Christian principles and precepts.

3. When it comes to pleasurable bad habits (eating too much), my last hurrah is always the last hurrah before the last hurrah.

4. Brief and very periodic stints of controlled mania when clean and sober feel really good and have no hangover...per se.

5. There are things I still have to do daily, even minutely at times, to stay sober and drug-free, one day at a time.

6. Some folks are going to resent what you do or don't do, no matter what it is or isn't.

7. There are many things, if not most, I will not know until I know.

8. One can do 99 things very well, and one well but not quite as well, and some folks can't help but key on the one.

9. Just because one is driven doesn't mean they get to drive.

10. During active addiction, I used to love getting high and looking at water; in Recovery, I love looking at water, which gets me high.

11. Nobody who owns private property wants to abolish private property, unless they have a lot of political juice and benefit monetarily from the abolition.

12. There is a serpentine line between marketing one's own business on social media and shining one's egotistically inclined butt; I fail often.

13   I can find a reason every new day to take a drink.

14   Dust to dust is a must, but it is heartbreaking for those left behind...

15   Praise an infant and he or she quickly figures out it means something.

16   Trying to help an addict if he or she isn't ready is like trying to catch a fish if they are not bitin' and hungry. Fish on, but don't be too frustrated if nothing bites.

17   No surprise that gratuity and grateful have etymological relations.

18   We never really think about where our carcass, remains, or ashes will be interred or memorialized until it's time to, too late, or it never happens.

19   I often speak in idioms spoken by an idiot signifying nothing, yet I speak...

20   I don't believe God ever intended, nor did our forefathers ever expect, for us to become such a demonstrably litigious nation.

21   If I am judged based on my judgments, then I judge myself to be in trouble.

22   If we have to control things, then we are likely not in control. The sadist tries to control because he's not in control.

23   Our judgments affect our behavior.

24   It never gets easy listening to good advice from tactless people, but it does often pay to heed it.

25   Cool is overrated.

26   The ruts in life are usually due to multiple causation.

27   We all wear uniforms, even when we don't.

28 If "We Are the World," then it is incumbent upon "the determiners" to determine where the world begins and ends.

29 I understand why the famous hide. I'm not famous; if I were, sadly, I would be intolerable.

30 Gracious goes a long way.

31 Those who say, "That's easy," rarely realize nothing is easy like Sunday morning!

32 I usually figure I am distinctly me—for good or ill—when fellow Christians don't think I'm strait-laced enough and non-Christians think I'm too "Christian."

33 The most important worldwide metric seems not to be based on accomplishment or outcomes, but popularity.

34 God is the Father of instinct.

35 Deficiencies inherent in the character of the social extremes are likely more easily evidenced than those found in the proverbial middle of the bell curve.

36 Malachi's quotes are primarily written for bright, reflective, inquisitive seekers.

37 Interesting first thought today at age 62: I pondered what would I be interested in knowing after I have departed this foil of a mortal coil; 'twas not if I would be remembered for any perceived accomplishments, but what would my children tell their children and possibly their grandchildren about me. Makes it worth trying to stay on the high (not high) road.

38 I'm either at the lake, on the lake, in the lake, near a lake, or thinking about a lake!

39   My telling a "white" lie to make a point is no different from those I disagree with who do the same.

40   Dreams can be prescient but usually void of discernible logic.

41   When my plethora of insecurities pop up en masse, I usually have acted in a way contrary to how I should live; I just often don't want to admit it.

42   As a recovering alcoholic, I no longer want a drink, but I still want to drink.

43   I talk about sobriety because it helps me stay sober.

44   In the Deep South, there are at least three types of friends: friends, dear friends, and "my friends." The first are friends, the second are close friends or those we claim as such, and "my friends" is the exclusive nomenclature of politicians, a bevy of pastors, and all grifters.

45   When hip trumps rectitude, the transcendental nature of the church and the individual is compromised.

46   Our soul is an oyster; our bed is the world; our morals begin as a single grain of sand within us.

47   Weight is often as subjective as it is factual.

48   Just telling folks to "Just Say No" to something that feels good without a succinct, empirical explanation in layman's terms is futile!

49   "Need," when it comes to kayaks, is in the eye of the luster.

50   I know it's not realistic to always have a "babe" in a cop/suspense drama…but it is easy on aging eyes.

51   It's difficult in today's social environment to trust anyone in the National spotlight who is vulnerable to blackmail, unless he or she allows the search for Truth to supersede reputation.

52 Living life outside the fence but in the wide-open suits a Delta boy.

53 "Don't have to be nowhere," doesn't mean nothin', but it does.

54 Buzzards are axiomatic: they stay hungry; therefore, they relish death.

55 How wonderful to really not worry about what specific people think about me: someday, maybe.

56 Just because a padre tells me from the raised dais to close my eyes while he prays or preaches, doesn't mean I'm going to; I usually pray more fervently with my eyes open.

57 Too many images stored—mental or otherwise—are detrimental to an expanding soul.

58 The strength of a conviction is never really known until tested by a conflagration.

59 A quick wit, though often dazzling, is not necessarily indicative of intelligence or common sense, for it surely stretches wisdom's membrane.

60 Some things are worth confronting; but a redneck patriot cleaning his weapons shirtless in the front yard with a case of PBR while listening to Skynyrd, after his old lady left him, he has shingles, and his favorite SEC team just loss a championship game to a Big Ten school, is not one of 'em.

61 When introverts assume the role of extrovert, it takes a toll on the soul.

62 A little alcohol is not necessarily a bad thing, unless a little is not enough.

63 Wisdom is the ongoing byproduct of intelligence and common sense after they've hooked up at finishing school.

64 In so many ways I'm still as fragile as my last day in active addiction, in some others, not as much.

65 Ill-mannered children become ill-mannered adults who have ill-mannered children.

66 Bitter anything is still bitter and usually distasteful.

67 Small beginnings are just the beginning and are not to be despised.

68 Privilege, in Uncle Sam's America, often lives at the societal extremes.

69 Alienation can be lonely, yet peaceful.

70 The lowest fella on the totem pole sure totes a lot of weight.

71 'Tis better to release a resentment with God's help than to bury it and hope it doesn't fester.

72 If someone is not as gracious as we want him or her to be, or as gracious as we believe ourselves to be, it's better not to engage in resentment, but to be thankful we know the difference.

73 Self-appointed outliers should rarely complain.

74 A lil woke can create empathy; a lot of woke can create mania.

75 At times, pleasant is enough.

76 There is so much tragedy in the world, and seemingly more every day.

77 The effect of death affects much.

78 We all have a date with death, but we do have input as to the final destination.

79 If the predominantly good guys with legal guns and the predominantly bad guys with illegal guns refuse to turn them in voluntarily—particularly during skyrocketing national crime rate increases coupled with law enforcement shortages—then it would be foolish for the layperson not to keep his for protection.

80 I didn't just know Cooter Brown; I was Cooter Brown.

81 I understand very little until I do.

82 Cult and "cultic" are not necessarily synonymous: one can be cultic while eschewing cults.

83 If God doesn't come back first, we will eventually revert the Earth back to the Stone Age, just with the addition of a bunch of broken toys and people.

84 A little notoriety can be a beautiful thing; too much notoriety can be suffocating.

85 I notice things about people, yet rarely am aware of things about things.

86 I'm on my own spectrum, no one will deny.

Chapter 20

1. It's imperative that I remember not all kids got Cheddar Goldfish, Cheese Whiz and pistachios on Christmas morning.

2. Even when on vacation, given the choice of "do" or "see," I always go with see; when the choice is "see" or "be," I always go with "be."

3. They don't call it Lake Superior for nothin': Gitche Gumee may not give up its dead, but it sure is a big blessing for the living.

4. When opposition is attenuated by apposition, harmony just might ensue.

5. The benefit of breaking bread with bright folks with a somewhat different worldview, who are also incredibly polite and thoughtful, is a beautiful thing.

6. Uber-ignorance is not, not knowing something, but a refusal to learn anything new.

7. Whatever we experience will likely tweak our vision and engender subtle changes in our lives.

8. My wife is truly a blessing: she lets me be stupid and allows me to self-discover my sheer stupidity.

9. I do, on occasion, enjoy posting something a little out there on social media just to smoke out the trolls hiding under the bridge.

10. If you are a prude, don't be rude.

11. Patronization is the new plantation.

12. 'Tis better to think how far we've come than fret how far to go; yet, better than both is to recognize and appreciate where we are.

13 I can be accused of a lot of things, and a whole lot of 'em are true.

14 I always choose "quiet," as it allows me to hear myself think better; however, therein lies the downside.

15 I still know less than I know, but more than I think.

16 When a politician or his mouthpiece consistently states, "we have been clear," they usually have not.

17 One must be securely insecure or insecurely secure to engage in constant self-deprecation.

18 To simply refer to the deceased as an heiress is dehumanizing.

19 A conspiracy theory is no longer a theory when it becomes a veritable, verifiable fact.

20 When overwhelmed by "ugly,"—personified and glorified, external and internal—it is a splendid idea for me to say nothing, while centering myself again—back on the water and in The Quiet!

21 When I get "caught up" in things inconsequential, I am caught, not caught up.

22 Just because folks helped me doesn't obligate me to agree with them when they are in the wrong; conversely, if they don't help me, I am still obligated to agree with them when they are in the right.

23 At times, I want to be alone, yet not alone.

24 I prefer George Washington Carver's definition of graft to that of a politician.

25 I have to keep my life simple—orderly, yet not too orderly—void of overstimulation, and God-centered, to stay sober, healthy and drug-free. Only God.

26 I believe in "Render unto Caesar what is Caesar's"; however, I do question what belongs to Caesar.

27 Failure learned can lead to success, but success breeds success.

28 Sometimes, a social media post just pulls the parasites out of the pork.

29 Regarding faith, we are limited only by our limitations.

30 Most foul things really are a rich man's trick.

31 Even if I live a lot longer, I'll be dead before I know it, if I even know it, unless this is not me.

32 It's not always enough to know what the right thing is.

33 Those who love money and power and who use hegemony and blackmail rule the world; yet, they do so under God's watchful eye.

34 God save the Queen and the shoulders and backs of those strappin' fellas totin' the lead casket up the chapel stairs!

35 It's coming.

36 God's promise to wipe away every tear is a big one.

37 As long as I stay in the present and look to the future, the past won't erode what remains.

38 When politicos, pundits, and piranhas mention "fair share," they are not including their portion.

39 It's never too late until it's too late to get right with our maker.

40 An observer is more passive than a watcher. I'm not a prophet, just a watcher.

41 History notes: Ivan doesn't lose! Just ask that lil Frog General with the original Napoleon complex.

42 Though I often refer to sweet alienation, it's really semi-sweet.

43 When I'm right, if I'm not kind, then I'm not right.

44 Had a girlfriend who once said she was mean as a snake; her eyes were elliptical; I believed her; I ran.

45 Full stadiums provide too many distractions.

46 The Heart of Darkness begins at the edge of darkness.

47 As an addict/alcoholic, I am not out of the woods as long as there is one tree left; but I love trees.

48 Corruption unchecked, yet observed, leads to apathy; corruption felt leads to antipathy.

49 I have an unparalleled ability to lose everything I touch.

50 I'm a marshmallow with a s'more crust.

51 One of the most myopic comments was made several years ago to my erstwhile kinsman, Chilly Billy Howell, when a local high-school-age girl told him she would love to take his regional-identity tour so she could learn about where she lived! Her Mom's comment: "Why would you want to do that; you are from here!"

52 Asking some politicians to sponsor an election-security bill is like asking a nursery of raccoons to guard the fish hatchery at night.

53 Carpetbags rarely carry carpets.

54 Shameful how often I try to be all things to all people, while publicly eschewing being all things to all people.

55 Bright is relative.

56 If I don't bring it, I'm going to need it.

57 Too often, a door opens another unwanted one.

58 To rhyme without rhyming is a difficult, yet beautiful thing.

59 A perma-buzz is still a buzz, for good or ill or both.

60 The biggest chore I ever had was balancing my buzz.

61 When you see a stop sign in the middle of nowhere, you know somebody had some juice.

62 Some folks are incapable of appreciating the nuances of complexity and the complexity of nuance.

63 Playing guitar with one's teeth may be unique and cool, but it will not change the world any more than my mentioning it.

64 Pastoral pompadours and barrister bouffants often speak volumes.

65 If Sobriety has changed my life as much as it has, imagine what a deeper Faith would do.

66 Business is not necessarily a service, and service is not necessarily a business.

67 The guise of freedom is a mask.

68 My biggest problem is I can't get enough.

69 I need a lot of quiet to be at Peace, and a lot of Peace to be quiet.

70 Relative and relevant are not synonymous, but can be parallel in the present.

71 Yom Kippur: To atone, we need to recognize we need to atone.

72 Saban is right; "rat poison," media praise, will kill you.

73 Whatever it is is likely better than what it wasn't.

74 Never believe a headcount unless you've counted heads.

75 If we compared vaccines to leaven, then it should at least cause one to question.

76 Just because we don't know who they are doesn't mean they aren't.

77 There is a cohesive duality between "I need help" and "I know what to do to get help and to help myself."

78 I'll just never understand Mamas letting their children grow up to be Bulldogs.

79 Politics is a shell game.

80 Recovery: Never easy, always worth it.

81 To mention crime is not politicizing crime.

82 Warmongers amaze me when they are amazed that the other side—because it's war—does what their side does.

83 If God spared not the martyrs, then I'm foolish to think I'm bulletproof.

84 Trying to find oneself is much better than not looking.

85 To be forgiven is better than not being forgiven, but it is not a free pass for licentiousness.

86 Cabal and offal may not rhyme, but they are kinfolks.

87 If cyanide is in rat poison and media praise is rat poison, then God protect the heralded.

88 What some see as patronization, many of us see as respect.

Chapter 21

1. I don't believe in spirit animals, but if I had one, it would be a narcissistic worm.

2. Fat folks and addicts like me have no business being in a buffet line.

3. How quickly the worm can turn from "I feel your pain" into "I am your pain!"

4. There is not much cuter than a happy, fat baby in a diaper!

5. I would think with all the back-scratching in politics that the backs of the takers and shakers should be bleeding like a stuck pig.

6. Clannish folks who refer to clannish folks astound me.

7. Tacky does as tacky is and tacky is as tacky does—vicious cycle of the insecure, small-minded.

8. Disengagement is the long-term result of one being ignored.

9. Unemployment rate and labor participation rate are not synonymous.

10. In old age and sobriety, I try not to commit or over-commit to anything I might not end up doing, accomplishing or attending. I am limited, and I have to set limits to remain sober and at peace.

11. In Recovery, I have to avoid the chronic, the tonic, and the toxic.

12. Cold weather is not cold until it gets here.

13. When I mitigate hyperbole, I get closer to the Truth.

14. Practicing the Presence of God is likely as passive as it is active.

15 Printing money and laundering money may make it funny money, but the non-launderers don't find it so funny.

16 If an adult's sole societal "contributions" are eating, peeing, crapping, whining, and sleeping, then that might qualify them as infantile.

17 After "seeing the world," and coming home to my Elephant's Graveyard, I find myself gravitating toward and shrinking "my world" to nature and my "homeboys!"

18 The gutless, spineless men who propagate the "Knockout Game" would be advised to keep that cowardly venture in New York City and out of rural America.

19 As I age, I try not to burn as many bridges, but it is not always easy.

20 When things are taken for granted and then disappear, there is usually a good reason.

21 I much prefer individuals to institutions and large groups.

22 The older I get, the more fervently I avoid toxic, life-suckers.

23 Just because modernity has edged closer to the Jetsons than the Flintstones, it doesn't mean Fred and Wilma don't still have a crack at the title.

24 There's always a reason; I just may not be aware of it.

25 Why? I just do what I do when I do it.

26 As I age, it behooves me to keep things where they belong, as I'll likely be able to find them when I surely lose them.

27 It's a sad day when the validity of peer reviews can no longer be trusted—follow the money.

28 Fighting Scripture with Scripture is rarely productive.

29   In Recovery, I have been continually rediscovering intimacy.

30   Just because my instincts are right doesn't make it the Truth.

31   Being a member of Mensa is not necessarily indicative of even a lick of common sense.

32   So much of what people held dear is dying because of what they now hold dear.

33   Societies on the margins, like people, are easy targets for carpetbaggers, scalawags, and grinning politicians who never met someone else's pocketbook they didn't covet.

34   I'm just a simple fella with good instincts who can be easily conned because I think I have good instincts.

35   What it's worth to me may not be what it's worth to you, but what it's worth to me determines what it's worth, if it belongs to me, whatever it is.

36   It's all "hard stuff" if it affects us.

37   In un-civil wars—aren't they all—when the Roundheads defeat the Royalists, the Roundheads become the Royalists.

38   Hegemony, politics, and raw power determine "fair share."

39   If I ever need more internal evidence that I am a fallen creature in need of beneficent help beyond the corporeal, I just remind myself how often I have to release resentments against people for things they haven't even committed yet, and likely never will.

40   Being a respecter of persons is an immutable snare, trying to please folks—friends, family, extended family, or unknowns—is fruitless; if they don't value you as you are, then they will likely not value what you would or could become.

41 I am an absolutist who sees the importance of duality in all things. To appreciate gestalt, one must find value in its discrete components.

42 Grace can be found in the most unexpected places.

43 White hats get dirty.

44 Gaining weight doesn't make me want to lose weight; losing weight makes me want to lose weight.

45 Hair is a trigger.

46 Native is relative.

47 Brusque doesn't work on foreign terrain.

48 Bottomless pits have no nadir.

49 Praise matters.

50 Often, the only hope I see in the natural world is the sweetness embodied in an innocent child; yet it breaks my heart for his or her future. Only God.

51 Part of my problem is I want to eat, yet I am not hungry.

52 They don't call it Crypto for no reason.

53 Basements may feel like dungeons, except basements usually have a manageable egress.

54 To adduce the Truth should not be inflammatory, yet it seems so today.

55 When talking has ceased, and veritable options are enervated, the Glasgow Kiss is often the only solution.

56 "The Widow's mite," spoken aloud, is a double entendre.

57   Never offend a writer if it can be avoided.

58   I don't take naps, not really; I just close my eyes and do some thinking.

59   I am thankful, with God's help, to have the capacity, if I will do so, to forgive others as I have been forgiven and would like to be forgiven.

60   The scar tissue from a mind flogging is hard to heal.

61   There are no fat folks playing international soccer.

62   Humor in the Mississippi Delta is more ubiquitous and certainly more necessary than raccoon roadkill.

63   Money helps, but an over-dependence on it leaves one hollow.

64   A desultory digression leads to depression.

65   Being an outlier has its advantages.

66   Recovery can be another addiction, albeit a healthier one.

67   I have difficulty learning without context or constructs.

68   When folks ask me, "Are you a . . .?" My answer depends upon how they define what they are asking.

69   Homophones, Arian and Aryan, are not synonymous by definition, nor are they easily defined in modern linguistics.

70   One can quickly find where he is in the pecking order contingent upon who answers personalized texts.

71   The means justify the end in God's economy, not vice-versa.

72   As a proverb raconteur, I try to share unusual thoughts to pique the interest of those who delight in self-discovery.

73 Understanding the complexities, continuity, and duality of the Mississippi Delta can be as difficult for a non-native as a soccer-loving neophyte has in understanding off-sides and yellow cards in fútbol.

74 It is not over until it's over, but it may be over.

75 The older I get, the more friends and acquaintances die; the more they die, the older I get.

76 The conceptual reality of time is beyond me; in fact, it befuddles me.

77 Even on good days, holidays are hard on addicts and alcoholics, whether in active addiction or Recovery.

78 When it comes to contests, I usually pull for the excellent, the familiar, or the underdog, but always for the most gracious—whether winner or loser.

79 For those in Recovery the winter holidays are doable, but sobriety can still be difficult—mentally and physically.

80 Reliving the past can be "a gas," but it's often fuel for a depressive conflagration.

81 When the Blue Monkey comes knocking at my holiday door, it helps for me to get out on the water in my kayak and to remember Michael Card's words: "human tears are older than the rain!"

82 If one has to ask, "Why are you depressed? You are so blessed!" they may have a good point, but they may not understand the nature and tenacity of depression.

83 Sobriety is hard enough when the sun is out, but it's a wee bit more difficult during the holidays.

84 When I'm needy, I tend to isolate, which is not necessarily a good thing.

85   The deeper the depression, the deeper the reflection.

86   Insecurities are ugly; I know, I have them.

87   "Misty Water Colored Memories" are not necessarily healthy for the depressingly reflective.

88   Amazing how many folks feel an obviously deep-seated need to tell me they disagree with me when their opinion hasn't been asked for, courted, or wanted.

89   Being raised by a good mama helps one become a good mama, but any woman can be a good mama.

90   As an addict, I have as hard a time not overdoing something healthy as I do something unhealthy.

Chapter 22

1. Tunes: I recognize them when I hear them, but I sure can't mimic or repeat them.

2. Jesus, as a winnower, does not fit the avuncular perception of those who misunderstand His great Love.

3. I had the amazing ability—nay, propensity—to eat everything set before me; and, it is still as challenging a daily choice not to do so, as it is not to take a drink.

4. Pygmalion pursuits are rarely long lasting, particularly if the preceptor has his own motives.

5. I'm so thankful there will be no child abuse or sex trafficking in Heaven.

6. The more we have, the more we have to have.

7. One good thing about being upset regarding a dissing by anyone is it reminds me how insanely sensitive I am.

8. Compartmentalization works, to an extent.

9. If being "successful" or authentic is important, one cannot hang with the peloton for long.

10. Unnatural highs are momentary and transitory.

11. Like the rules or not, it's the game.

12. The route I take is no more predictable than I am.

13. I don't like calling them demons anymore; I prefer "challenges!" I don't want to give the devil more than his due.

14. Let something mean something to me, and I might do something about it.

15. I'm very confident I would not remain stoic if tortured.

16. When the desire for fun puts us under the gun, it's time to run.

17. Boredom is a healthy diet's worst friend.

18. Artificial intelligence, photo-altering technology, and corruption make everything suspect.

19. I need to revisit the Beatitudes daily so that I'll be reminded not to "bow up" when vexed.

20. Glad begets glad.

21. When buzzards circle, I still pinch myself, just to be sure.

22. Ole Man River tolerates a few but answers to none.

23. I can't see the future, but I do have a few ideas about what it will look like.

24. I react.

25. Just when I'm proud of myself for a particular, yet-rare display of good behavior toward others…BAM…I quickly act a fool again.

26. Being proud of pride leads to more pride, which can be a pitfall for those realizing the necessity of humility in spirituality.

27. There is not much more beautiful and irenic than an abbey of monks chanting.

28. Bottom line: I don't want anybody telling me what I "have" to do.

29. If Lady Justice is blind, it might be time to open her eyes.

30   An addict can always find a silver lining; we have to to survive the consequences of our poor behavior predicated on our unresolved character defects.

31   Mamas don't let your redneck husbands dress your Shih Tzu hounds named Dandy in early morning below-zero weather for a potty break at a fancy hotel. The lobby ladies just may not understand.

32   Modern toilets with bidets and slow-close seats have spoiled my butt rotten.

33   Concealed Carry doesn't end at the door of even an elegant hotel in a safe city!

34   It's not possible to compartmentalize lust; it's pervasive and hungry.

35   Spiritual sense and spiritual sensibility are not always congruent, but it's a blessing when they harmonize.

36   Christ is positional; Jesus is personal; Jesus Christ is holistic.

37   I tried the box; I didn't like it.

38   When we have to question what we see and if it's "real" anymore, we are in trouble.

39   My wife displays spiritually what I understand cognitively but desire to attain spiritually.

40   There is no Heaven on Earth. There is only Earth and the Hope of Heaven.

41   The older I get, the only thing I seem to remember is what I forgot.

42   The lake is my cathedral, the kayak my pew, nature my lodestar, and God is my God.

43   The world is shallow.

44 Addiction is how I dealt with the past; in Recovery, I have to remember that it is past.

45 When Ma'am and Sir become a slur, society — or the lack of it—is in trouble.

46 The devil drives; the Lord guides.

47 It is understandable not to be able to understand the incomprehensible.

48 Though not alone, I still feel the felt of the lonely.

49 For an introvert, I tend to live life out loud.

50 Sometimes I hug, sometimes I don't; it depends.

51 Each addict's cocktail is a volatile batch.

52 If we think things are just things, then we sure do focus a lot on things.

53 We have to be awakened before wooed.

54 My roots need water, my head air, my heart cleansing, my feet washing, my hands salve, my back burden-lifting, my neck yoke-removing, my mind freeing—guided by Love.

55 There should be no average anybody; every walk is unique, or should be.

56 Commitments stress me.

57 I'm not a religious nut, but I'm comfortable with "spiritual nut."

58 Cool is at enmity with Christ.

59   We may remember a man's name and fame, but it does him no good when dead.

60   Though a person be dead, and his or her fame and name may no longer serve to assist, the remembrance of his good, her conviviality, or simply a fleeting frozen smile in time may augur Hope for who remains.

61   I hate for anybody to be lonely.

62   I can't be anybody else, nor should I try.

63   Regarding media, I enjoy brief flits with suspense, alienation, conundrums, and puzzles, but I eschew terror and raw evil.

64   The difference between the American Dream and a Kingdom Dream might just lie in the focus.

65   Amends don't always make friends.

66   Many people retain so much; I retain so little, fluid excluded.

67   Politics is like making sausage, except it smells worse.

68   Anonymity protects notoriety.

69   Some folks clown too much when a clown has not been ordered.

70   My blind spots are completely opaque.

71   God often squeezes us into a bigger place.

72   I'm a simple man limited to thought.

73   In sobriety, I am proof you can teach an old dog new tricks, but they need to be simple and at a slow pace.

74   Most of life and progress is about traction.

75   Latent responders still respond.

76   My response to the unfathomably miraculous should be sheer, child-like awe.

77   What we consistently view is what we embrace, and what we embrace is what we view.

78   The outcome, even if beneficial, of an unjustified action does not justify the action.

79   My wife, being present with God and His creation, is animating me to become more present with God and others.

80   Boredom is the addict's Achilles.

81   Every second spent with my wife is a gift.

82   Turgidity can only lead to fluidity if a membrane is pierced.

83   Unimaginative devolutionists are among us.

84   Butt sniffin' is only appropriate and efficacious in politics and the canine world.

85   At my age, if I don't see someone often enough, I likely may not remember his name on the spot.

86   Transmogrification is a big word, yet simple to understand, as it always involves a constant—change.

87   Modernity is as transient as billowing waves on wind-swept waters.

88   We live in an age where being "right," even if wrong, is more important than Truth.

Chapter 23

1. I have no greater joy in life than spending time, daily, with my wife talking about things that matter, should matter, could matter, or even the inconsequential things, which really don't matter...but they do, if spent in the presence of one who matters.

2. I am consistently amazed at social media warriors who enjoy posting ad hominem attacks on party members not from their party—even if true—yet give the grotesque transgressions of those within their identified political party a full pass.

3. I often feel this once great nation and beacon of hope, Truth, and freedom is heading downhill on a 20-degree grade without even a handbrake, and we are more concerned about the state of a shrew than the chasm waiting to consume us.

4. Me going to Mardi Gras as a recovering addict would be like chunking Brer Rabbit in the briar patch.

5. Three things still make my heart skip a beat: the sight of my wife after a brief absence; sunsets in my kayak on Moon Lake; and, though sober, flashing blue lights while driving.

6. I pray for the recall of the things I know, and the wisdom to know the things I don't.

7. Lusting after anything is fruitless, but lusting after a memory tops them all.

8. Visiting is good for me, but it takes a lot out of me.

9. Hard and slimy are not antithetical when it comes to describing reptiles and those whose actions are reptilian.

10. The shame of a battle lost must not define the war.

11. I want to scream, "treason, no reason, whom are we pleasing?" from the rooftops; yet, I write poetry.

12. Treason is not just political.

13. I am often as bemused as I am amused, and often at the same time.

14. I'm thankful my wife appreciates and understands my limitations, as they are legion.

15. The beautiful, yet stark alienation in winter quietly displays rarely seen matter in poignant contrast to the verdant Southern summer.

16. Writing poetry has been my growing-out-of-latency response to a continual awareness and appreciation for God's Kingdom in the now and in the forever.

17. My favorite and most inspiring theologian is a singer/songwriter.

18. Amazon is an addict's nightmare.

19. My plan to eat less during the winter as I move less appears to be fraught with obstacles.

20. Overused, spiritual platitudes go in one ear and out the other! Original, authentic thoughts are more palatable and infinitely easier to receive and digest.

21. If men are pigs and women are figs, may the boar never eat sweets.

22. I hate "big box" stores almost as much as I use them.

23. It's not that I stay hungrier than the next fella; it just takes me longer to get filled up.

24. 'Tis better to judge none by his or her strengths.

25. I seem adept at offending the really religious and the irreverent.

26 Telling folks we are fond of them, if we really mean it, is endearing.

27 If I'm ever selected by an haute couture magazine as "the sexiest man alive," I'm turning down the honor because I don't want to be objectified.

28 Foul looks as foul is as foul does.

29 Victimization is the devil's Roman arena, where one-armed gladiators wait to die.

30 My addict brain was always defensive while being offensive.

31 If I can forgive and release a resentment I have against someone I see often, because I see him or her often, I sure should forgive someone who offended me 20 years ago.

32 The "one-eyed man in the land of the blind," may be king. but blind must first be defined.

33 I am constantly amazed at the sorry folks who resent nice folks because they are nice and not sorry.

34 I try to avoid political discussions except within the confines of my own home.

35 I love cigar lounges where conversation, erudition, jocularity and authenticity reign supreme.

36 I seem to get into even more trouble trying to be who I'm not than being who I am.

37 Being sad hearing about all the abuse of children is not the same as being sad hearing about it and then figuring out with God's help what I am to do about it.

38 Everybody's crazy; some of us are just better at it than others.

39 Fast does often augment smart.

40 The devil might have gone down to Georgia, but he didn't stop there…

41 I can't fight in every arena of need, but in the one or two I'm supposed to, Lord, let me know where they are, what to do and not do, and then give me strength and favor.

42 Cupid's cupidity might pit love against mammon.

43 When a member from an older generation, who is "in her cups" at night, tells me, meaning well, that she just wants me to be "successful," I do believe it might just be intimating that I am not.

44 I prefer a backpack to a briefcase—always have.

45 There's a lot more down a rabbit hole than a fluffle of bunnies.

46 Sinning takes a lot out of you, and more than just the Good.

47 "No stress" even stresses me.

48 When the past encroaches on the present, the future just might be in trouble.

49 Marie may have said, "let 'em eat cake," but the nouveau elite will be happy when we see the return of the Hoovervilles; will not be a chicken in every pot, either.

50 It's all meaningless if it doesn't have meaning.

51 Redemption matters to a life in tatters.

52 Manifest Destiny is simply destiny determined largely by those who manifest the most power and are not afraid to use it.

53   "They" get away with whatever they want because they get away with whatever they want.

54   Some things are simply too simple to be understood.

55   Sadly, the greatest Love most people recognize and truly experience is that of a faithful dog.

56   "Clean cut" is not necessarily synonymous with Holy or honest.

57   If Jesus was a Man of sorrows, I reckon it's okay for me to be sad--as long as I don't wallow too long--when I see the devolution of humanity engulf a world in tatters.

58   I struggle with death, when I'm not conveniently dismissing it due to its temporal finality.

59   Given the convolutions and serpentine synapses in my brain, without God I would be more fractured than a broken kaleidoscope.

60   When I'm flat emotionally, I need to always be sure I don't leave my keys within the devil's reach.

61   Philosophizing can be a lonely endeavor.

62   A jellied brain is the devil's playground.

63   Blood may be thicker than water and water more pervasive than blood, but the Spirit is stronger and more omnipresent than both.

64   Every person, a camera; every person, a phone; every person, a computer; but, still there is not a chicken in every pot.

65   Often, I have to understand things to understand things.

66 Regarding the Biblical admonition to be, "wise as serpents, but as innocent as doves," that first part is a lot easier for a fallen creature like me than the second part.

67 I'm not who I was, so I shouldn't act like I did.

68 To understand Dixie, one must appreciate duality!

69 "Falsus in uno, falsus in omnibus" may not be true all the time, but it does not behoove to discredit entirely.

70 Strong as a cedar and flexible as a palm. Lord, help me be, 'cause I am not.

71 Lyre and liar may be homophones, but they have very different melodies.

72 How often we dogmatically believe what we've heard, but not what we see.

73 "Reasonable" is subjective.

74 The numinous Elmer Gantry is among us: buyer beware.

75 Thinking is a large part of my job.

76 Beginnings are often the best.

77 People should not hate Russians for loving their Motherland any more than they should hate Southerners for loving Dixieland.

78 We have ruined the World with busy.

79 I have no problem being distracted by distractions.

80 I'm not a great cook, but what I do cook, I cook well.

81 For the alcoholic, the blessings of sobriety always outweigh the perceived benefits of another drink; yet perception often wins.

82 One may use an addict, but it's difficult to con one.

83 All of my insecurities are rooted in insecurity.

84 Lockstep Louie is full of phooey.

85 "Beware the Ides of March" is not confined to one day a year. Shun the obsequious.

86 I think more than I do; yet do more than I think, I think.

87 There is no respect like the respect from the folks I most respect.

88 The practicality and spiritual principles endemic in Recovery taught me how to begin putting feet to my Faith.

89 Sticking to schtick may be expedient, easy and quick, but it does limit spontaneity.

Chapter 24

1 Too much work stifles a philosopher.

2 Dogma is death.

3 When a tree frog sings, the whole body, including the leg and diaphragm, get involved.

4 Where I'm from matters, but not as much as who I am.

5 Corporeal is tangible; spiritual is not, unless it is.

6 It doesn't take a washtub full of imagination to ascertain how the estrangement of a loved one affects one.

7 If I'm ashamed for being full of pride, then I should not be full of pride for being ashamed.

8 The fruit of the Spirit has many manifestations, but it all comes from the same Tree.

9 All my thoughts are original, even if they aren't; conversely, all my thoughts are not original, even if they are.

10 The thinner the membrane, the more it might matter.

11 A possibility for many is a Truth for some.

12 I used to get high when depressed; drink when delirious; now, I struggle with eating when bored…or, awake.

13 Deep affectation occurs when distant memories become wispy, spectral feelings.

14 Scarring moments are slashes on canvas, indelible, time the only salve and blotter.

15 All roots music may embody pain as a catalyst, but it is best expressed and found in cultures and communes where the simple life includes time and inclination to express that pain and an appreciation for one's terroir.

16 I love a physical swamp, but a metaphorical one is the bane of first-world living.

17 If the "glory days" didn't kill me, then thinking about 'em too much just might.

18 The power of wind can be foe or friend, but the unseen often becomes the seen.

19 There's always a reckoning just around the corner.

20 Ritual is important in my Faith, yet I too often rely on it for my Faith.

21 It is not always easy to define legitimate.

22 When a society devolves into governance by kangaroo courts, the commonwealth has disintegrated.

23 To celebrate classlessness, regardless of justification, is a step in the wrong direction.

24 When pragmatism trumps Truth, every institution is imperiled.

25 The longer I live, the more I refrain from unpleasant dialogue; my own internal monologue, not so much, because I don't fear my own reprisal.

26 Pragmatism is a short-term solution to a long-term problem.

27 I avoid ex cathedra, not because I am so pure, but quite the opposite.

28 When hyperbole accompanies tragedy, the true impact is often diminished.

29 The only Assurance I have in this life is One I can't see.

30 Geese are infinitely more monogamous than human beings.

31 Scars and scar tissue change things.

32 Looking at things correctly is not always the right way to look at things.

33 What's true doesn't always represent the Truth.

34 I'm a mess with my wife, but a bigger, hot mess without her.

35 Being sober around sober people can make one less likely to drink or more likely to drink.

36 Be humble and shut up is the best advice I never listen to.

37 When not in a good place, I often don't really know why, though I usually think I know why, but I do know what to do about it, whether I will or not.

38 Folks who tint their windows—physically and metaphorically—should never get upset when the world doesn't wave.

39 Justified anger does not always equate to righteous anger.

40 Lust, pride, and bitterness are the bane of the would-be-righteous.

41 The paradox inherent in one of the most often written commands in the Bible—Fear the Lord—is, yes we should, and no, we shouldn't; yet, we better…

42   Coercion creates dispersion.

43   Being present with the present is a present my wife shares with me every day.

44   A slippery slope is best recognized before the slide.

45   To not watch the intros to Law and Order and The Office, even if seen a 1,000 times, is like skipping dinner when you're hungry or turning your back on an old friend.

46   Often, I don't want to ask the opinion of loved ones and friends regarding what I say and do, not because I don't care, but because I do.

47   It's a crying shame the #METOO movement didn't envelop, hedge, and seek to protect boys, girls, and trafficked individuals.

48   I am what I am, and I do what I do, if others don't like it, that's alright too.

49   The World is rumbling—the beginning of tremors.

50   I don't tell Malachi what to say.

51   I often forget that I was "fearfully and wonderfully made"; it's just a shame what I did with God's masterpiece.

52   If I was a fool then, I'm likely a fool now.

53   I don't discuss politics with people who hold a polarized worldview, and I surely don't do it if I care about them.

54   Only Artificial Intelligence doesn't have Mommy issues.

55   When overwhelmed, I occasionally wake up in the wee hours of the morning dragging baggage that God rid me of years ago.

56 As the world turns, so does the worm--quickly, and often without notice.

57 Even when I don't want to see it coming, I'd rather see it coming.

58 An upside to giving gifts twice to folks who don't say thanks is they aren' given for the thanks.

59 The freedom to do it grants me the freedom not to do it.

60 With low to no expectations, I'm usually pleasantly surprised.

61 If I don't know what to get people I like what they like, I get them what I like that I think they'll like.

62 Statistically, and in life, reliable consistency is not the same as consistent reliability.

63 I don't vote in "contests" where one can vote more than once; that's an aberrant popularity contest signifying very little.

64 Memories are just that.

65 Very little feels better than not feeling bad, after feeling bad.

66 How a society decides anything is how it decides everything.

67 I might ask for the sale, but I am not going to push for it.

68 I get addicted to things that are not even addictive.

69 I can get lost and lonely again "real quick" without God.

70 Times have never been as innocent as they seem to be in retrospect.

71 Sometimes, I just have to emote out loud: I am so thankful to be sober and married to Madge.

72 There are very few sentient beings more obnoxious than a female cowbird.

73 Occasionally, what doesn't work might work, but most of the time, what doesn't work doesn't work.

74 Were Thoreau still around, I fear he would find our lives of "quiet desperation" not so quiet, yet still very despairing.

75 Who and what we find beautiful are not always what others expect.

76 My thoughts are mostly original, yet most likely inspired by the thoughts of others.

77 Put me through the wringer; there will be nothing left.

78 I kinda like not always knowing what day it is.

79 I agree it is likely a sin to kill mockingbirds, but they can be as mean as yard dogs and wet hens.

80 When my wife said her Daddy never judged her, it made me think.

81 I may have to keep moving at times and my leg never stops shaking, but I am pretty sure I don't qualify as a mover and a shaker.

82 Anybody can be canceled.

83 There are still times I have to remind myself that everyone in my orb doesn't appreciate me or maybe even like me, and that it is okay.

84 There is a notable difference between attention and the right kind of attention.

85 Breaking bread facilitates empathy.

86 Having given up alcohol and substance abuse, I am likely down to just one diagnosis.

87 The inestimable value of a wife who allows her husband to be brutally vulnerable——then assiduously protects that hedge-less vulnerability——is incalculable.

88 As a youngster, reading Twain, I always thought Tom was brilliant attending his own funeral; now, as an old man, I'm perfectly okay not hearing what folks say about me.

Chapter 25

1. Until we feel pain from the very policies we promote or ignore, which create pain for others, nothing will change.

2. There is cool, and then there is Simon Templar cool, or Bob's not my Uncle.

3. Until "it" hits home, it's merely theoretical.

4. Even the chosen have to choose.

5. I have been redeemed—eternally and temporally—but make no mistake, I am damaged goods.

6. When overwhelmed with any sort of grief, I have a habit of revisiting all of my life failures.

7. I rarely want a drink anymore; I rarely don't want a drink anymore—duality!

8. The children of Israel were in Egypt 400 years or so, in the desert 40 years or so, America has been a hot mess for several generations—the worm turns slower than many of us would like.

9. When the Law can defy the Law then the institution is lost and all it was designed to protect.

10. Fight Truth long enough and it becomes unrecognizable.

11. I have to work hard kayaking and eating right just to stay fat.

12. God forgave me for who I was; I pray He forgives me for who I am and will be, and that He will help me forgive myself as well.

13   'Tis truly a sad day when so many in the world believe that Christians who hold a more traditional, orthodox view of scripture and its historical influence upon Judeo-Christian ideology/theology are evil, racist, mean-spirited and hateful.

14   Heaven is the endless Presence of God.

15   It's rather easy to hate on what we don't understand or want to understand.

16   Fear of the Lord is antithetical to fear.

17   Much is realized in the silence.

18   We live so fast we often don't recognize fear as a prime motivator.

19   "They" are trying to destroy the middle class with busy.

20   A sense of urgency is a double-edged sword.

21   I don't know how God did it, but He did it.

22   Reelect can be a good thing, a bad thing, or just a thing.

23   Even cynics can be duped.

24   If the answer is blowin' in the wind, then it behooves me to keep walking.

25   As an introvert, one way to truly protect my introversion is by often performing as an extrovert.

26   I've spent more time with me than anybody else.

27   The end of eras and epochs is easier to take sentimentality–wise the older and more tired I get.

28 There is a difference between going in a door and the door coming to us.

29 My ripe old age, at best, is closer than I imagine and getting riper by the moment.

30 Disparate treatment will never balance scales.

31 If love is a choice and "in love" is a feeling, then being in love with love should lead to a choice.

32 When I resent others for resenting others, I am no different than the others who resent others.

33 Encouraging others who don't encourage me is difficult, but important.

34 I need to be more of a healer and less of a feeler.

35 Little disappoints me more than disappointing my wife and girls, though they graciously and rarely telegraph disappointment.

36 It shouldn't matter what others think of me, unless I give them just cause to think negatively.

37 I spent many painful and fruitless years unknowingly—mostly—resenting God for not fixing what I didn't see coming, but in which I played a role.

38 If my Daddy hadn't been Roundman and I wasn't Lil Round, I could have been a rawboned contender.

39 He who plants a saguaro cactus takes a long view.

40 Watching others celebrate Father's Day is difficult.

41 The First-World problems I deal with and stew over are really rather silly given my blessings.

42   Being overwhelmed with worry about being overwhelmed is overwhelming.

43   When I change my thinking from "have to" to "get to," my whole world improves.

44   If I don't live up to your expectations, please remember, they are your expectations.

45   I do shift gears, but there is usually an uncomfortable grind in between.

46   I know personalized license plates will never have more than seven characters, yet count I still.

47   Every time I travel back home into the Delta—Mississippi, Arkansas, or Louisiana—I sigh for happy.

48   The spontaneity of originality can't be manufactured, even casually.

49   I'll never lose weight if I keep justifying one last hurrah.

50   God doesn't belong in a box. He doesn't fit.

51   I'm not yet comfortable in my own skin, but I do become more so every year; maybe, by the time the old epidermis is completely desiccated, I'll be so.

52   Casuistic Humanism is antithetical to Theism, deism, and belief in transcendence.

53   I spend more time wanting God to please me than I do trying to please God.

54   We can be as colorful as we want to be as we get older because we care less what others think.

55   My wife loves the Lord; therefore, she loves others and me.

56   Entrenched, often-inherited, ideology not predicated on Truth will ultimately destroy any and all organizations, from nations to churches to families.

57   Sinecure may be secure, but it secures no crowns in Heaven.

58   It is not a trial if it is not painful.

59   Love leads to obedience, and obedience intensifies love.

60   Evil spirits are rapacious in their pursuit of those dealing with mental illness or addiction.

61   I don't have anything against chocolate labs, but as a rule, many are living proof Albert Schweitzer didn't breed with canines.

62   I look forward to Eternity, mysterious and unknown; yet I fear it a little, only because it's unknown. I struggle with even the known unknown; however, I believe God when He says it will be glorious.

63   Nobody is colorblind unless they are colorblind.

64   Knowing better and doing better are not the same thing, but one should lead to the other.

65   For the believing believer, Eternity is the known unknown.

66   God has always had a remnant.

67   Manufactured experiences are still experiences, yet they are still manufactured.

68   The white drone of a river barge is cathartic, even on a river intrinsically silent.

69   Many situations should be viewed as "situational" not personal.

70   The mysteries of Faith include: we choose; yet, we are chosen.

71 Beware tapered haircuts bearing promises too good to be true.

72 Forgiveness is the oil of goodwill.

73 Looking "clean-cut" doesn't always equal clean cut.

74 My truth is not necessarily the Truth.

75 One blueberry just picked tastes sweeter than a handful gobbled.

76 Going to the movie theater on a rare occasion when training for a race and knowing I have to pass on the nachos, popcorn, and soda is as stressful as attending your first cocktail party sober, post-treatment.

77 You know you are tender when half your suitcase is pillows and a stuffed frog and you are 65 years old.

78 The future is fairly predictable if we neglect admonishments and lessons that should have been learned from the past.

79 Hope without Faith holds no water.

80 Progress at all costs is progress all lost.

81 Southern man cannot live on watermelon alone, but I do give a yeoman's crack at the title as often as possible.

82 If watermelon is a drug, then consider me in relapse.

83 The advent of the "Big Gulp" cup was not advantageous for the addict.

84 My "just enough" is not your just enough.

85 Logos speak.

86   "I'll believe it when I see it" and "I'll see it when I believe it" tango well together.

87   The most served are not always the over-served.

88   Once one starts "feeling" spiders, it's hard to stop feeling them.

89   Sometimes, just being semi-retired is a full-time J. O. B.; don't hate, percolate!

Chapter 26

1. I didn't smile a lot when heavy sodden with booze and depression and living a demonstrably unhealthy lifestyle.

2. I prefer mentally complex to mentally ill—my capricious mind approves this message.

3. Just because I'm selfish doesn't mean I'm good to myself.

4. The "good ole boy" system is not relegated to just good old boys.

5. The oxymoronic symbiosis of routine plus varied life experiences helps one stay progressive yet grounded.

6. Pressing conversation with the reticent is uncomfortable for both parties.

7. My empathy increases when I try to look at others through my limited understanding of God's eyes, instead of my sin-stained, occluded lenses.

8. There are those who are cool and work at it; those who are cool and don't work at it; and, those who could not care less about cool, now that's cool.

9. The world seems to become less fluid day by day.

10. There are no wasted trips for the thankful.

11. Anything that robs me of peace should be questioned.

12. I don't covet the favor of those who dispense favor only to those who seek their favor.

13. Don't fear doing it; just do it.

14   Every child is a pearl of great price.

15   "Blind" eyes often hide lies; overt lies often belie blind eyes.

16   Lust robs us of more than Holiness; it robs us of time.

17   My good intentions are more thought-to-be good intentions than I realize.

18   The less I think ill of others, the more likely I will think that they think less ill of me than I think they do.

19   Vitriol replacing dialogue effectively eliminates dialogue and leads to monologue.

20   A nose stuck way up in the air is less likely to smell the roses, as is one close to ground.

21   As narratives transmogrify, due to necessity, some things become more generalized while others become more specific.

22   My world, this world, gets smaller day-by-day.

23   If I struggle with being kind because it is not native to my nature, then I should be kind because it is God's nature.

24   A sense of place is defined by the generalized and specific grace and pace.

25   I need to shave more often with Hanlon's Razor: "Never attribute to malice that which is adequately explained by stupidity."

26   The New World Order is the problem.

27   I don't understand, but when I understand that I don't understand, I understand.

28 In watching old action movies, I realize that the karate chop and chloroform have come a long way.

29 If we must trust something of value to someone, it might behoove us to trust it to someone we don't mind stealing it.

30 Grumbling does not please God.

31 The silence to the fast-approaching, universal, public push for the acceptance of pedophilia as a viable relationship option is staggering.

32 My brain, like silly putty, kneaded and stretched slowly, produces a more usable, pliable substance; too quickly, it squirms like Morrison's toad.

33 The devolution of culture: Cool became more important than tradition after tradition had become more important than Truth.

34 Humility can defrost even the most frigid of hearts.

35 Rivers, and those who paddle them, can humble one in an instant.

36 There is not much commonality between being the G.O.A.T and a goat.

37 The world needs more order, but it doesn't need a New World Order.

38 Often, the "hardest" people are the most sensitive; they've just grown a crustacean's shell.

39 Camelot is magical, until it is not.

40 I'm thankful for family and friends who recognize my plethora of limitations and make grand allowances for them.

41 When discussion about bowel movements supersedes discourse regarding fine women and football, a fella just might be considered past prime.

42 Goodbyes have always been very difficult for me; I often have to block out or bury the devastation.

43 Still wondering whether or not someone believes I am telling the truthful truth reminds me I have not always, and still do struggle with it.

44 A critical spirit is not indicative of prophetic gifting.

45 I'm relational; I just can't handle too much communication.

46 I was born out of time, yet at the right time.

47 I love subcultures despite and because of their general and specific peculiarities.

48 Take advantage of the passive/aggressive and one doesn't get the passive.

49 Painful and productive are not always antithetical.

50 The only thing the Christian is left with in the long haul is his relationship with the Lord––all else dies or fades away.

51 I need to learn to say, "no," without being ugly and without feeling guilty for saying "no." I know, "No!" is a complete sentence; yet, I too often feel a need to explain.

52 The more a talker talks the less I listen.

53 Producing green energy sucks chlorophyll.

54 I'm better than I used to be, but not nearly as good as I ought to be, or hope to be.

55 Holding resentment equals punishing those who are unaware they are being punished—because they aren't—yet it punishes the punisher.

56 When something tastes good, I always think more is better, until it isn't.

57 Having everything can mean nothing, and having nothing can mean everything.

58 As a generalization, buying, selling or trading among friends has the potential to create resentments and damage friendships.

59 Pride is not cheap.

60 I know just enough about it to stay out of it.

61 I don't fit anywhere, and above the surface, I don't care.

62 I've always thought too highly of myself, while knowing I was a worm.

63 Recognition without joy is detrimental to the soul.

64 The invisible tension between folks can be one of the most tangible intangibles or intangible tangibles.

65 One upside to my sharing with others evidence of my potty mouth is I am usually instantly convicted and reminded how far I need to go to be pleasing to God.

66 It's staggering how often others knowing my misdeeds will convict me, yet I will not acknowledge any conviction by the Holy Spirit.

67 Bad memories entertained and fostered still have the power to destroy me.

68 Replacing scriptural orthodoxy with progressive idealism is a plank worth treading lightly on.

69 A man not only has to know his limitations, he has to set some limitations.

70 One has to be miserable to act miserable.

71 The past keeps me from being present; yet, being present keeps the past in check.

72 I tend to avoid places where I find it hard to be myself or where others find it hard for me to be myself.

73 Yankees are often an invasive species.

74 To the addict, anything less than a cup is just about a teaspoon.

75 It's hard to put a premium on peace; there is no premium on Peace.

76 I am the problem...I AM is the Answer...

77 Five years drug-free and sober, and I better not take whiskey or the craving numbness of a buzz for granted.

78 45 years ago, when I was 18 and wearing Ray-Ban Aviators, the world was my oyster; I just didn't realize cultured pearls were so rare.

79 Little makes me more joyful than a happy baby; little makes me sadder than an unhappy baby.

80 Having lost and kept off over 65 pounds in the last few years, I am finally the weight I've been lying about for over 40 years. The Truth just took me a long time.

81 My favorite conversation starter with friends and acquaintances who are readers is, "What are you reading now?"

82 It's one thing to know about Orwell's "1984"; it's another thing to read it slowly and intentionally.

83 If you hear I went on a hunger strike, it is not the truth.

84 There can be a wide chasm between being a good, Christian counselor and a good-Christian counselor.

85 Lord, I can't do it without you, even though I often think I can.

86 The future is largely unknown, and for that I am usually very grateful.

87 Live long enough in this media-driven, instant-gratification, techno-proficient world and scandal will eventually find most of us.

Chapter 27

1. Thin, lean, and firm are not always synonymous.

2. Overlooking others' wrongs is vital for spirituality, and is something I struggle with; however, it is often too easy to overlook my own wrongs.

3. Faith's known unknowns lend credence to the Mystery.

4. Those of us who experience and even seek alienation for a multitude of obvious and unrecognizable reasons still relish an invitation to "belong."

5. If I don't fully remember you, it's not your fault.

6. Wisdom is the application of knowledge, and right action is wisdom in deed.

7. The ease with which we seemingly accept death with so little contemplation astonishes me.

8. When taking a deep, long, slow breath, it can be difficult to imagine a lifetime of them.

9. Sighing is often my go-to regulator.

10. In God's presence, I am diminished, yet not...

11. Jesus is extreme.

12. Hope deferred is not preferred, but it is still hope.

13. The past is as present as I allow.

14 The innocence of a young daughter post-bath in her nightgown sitting next to Dad reading a storybook is difficult to replicate.

15 When the worm turns, it doesn't ask permission.

16 I may say today something I'll have to correct tomorrow.

17 When it comes to food, salt should be a friend, not a lover.

18 Being a servant should not be a pejorative.

19 At times, I still have to remind myself not to toot my horn every time I blow my nose.

20 I hate when I lack the energy to exercise but have ample to eat like it's my last meal on death row.

21 Please God, but I sure get in the way on The Way.

22 Friday-late-afternoon missives from an ex-anybody are rarely a blessing.

23 Be like a visitor. Be happy to be here.

24 If I pick up one more book to read that I already read in the last few months, and forgot about, I might need to check myself in to an insane asylum.

25 To pray for the Peace of Jerusalem is a Biblical command; to want peace in Jerusalem is a human imperative.

26 If it is not personal, it often is not real.

27 The invisible strings of unseen puppet masters are ties that bind as surely as cords of steel.

28   It's taken me a lifetime to even begin realizing I don't need to apologize and draw attention to what I'm apologizing for that doesn't even need an apology.

29   Some people thrive and feel most alive when dealing with stress; I am not one of 'em.

30   When rich folks give money to good causes, it's admirable and appreciated; when poor folks give money, the heavens roar with jubilation.

31   Solemnity in service is important, but it can be taken too far.

32   If I don't call, don't take it personally; I hate a telephone.

33   A little Truth in the mouth of a fool is still Truth, but it can be dangerous when poorly dispersed.

34   Smart and cunning are not always synonymous.

35   Over five years clean and sober and I still miss whiskey. Sobriety will continue to be a daily decision until my last breath, but one worth making.

36   A heart without honor does not beat quite right.

37   When paddling in adverse weather I have to remind myself that no pain in training leads to poor results when racing.

38   God owes me nothing.

39   Humility goes a long way.

40   I must often count my mind as being the enemy.

41   When doves scream for war, there is decomposition in Denmark.

42 I don't necessarily believe in skin walkers, nor in shape shifters; however, I do believe predatory hawks can masquerade as mourning doves.

43 Life often frightens me, then I remember...

44 Tragic, how often I am praying and unholy things enter my mind.

45 I paralyze too easily.

46 As an addict, I now view my daily reading of Proverbs through an addict's eyes, and they now mean more to me than they did before.

47 The reason the excessive behavior of Young Turks irritates me is because I was one.

48 I like wearing worn things since I don't worry about wearing them out.

49 Subtlety matters in cooking and living.

50 I'm happy not overdoing anything that I don't overdo, and overdoing anything that is not unhealthy.

51 "Over-news" is no news.

52 Filtered sunlight late in the day on a brisk fall or winter afternoon never fails to holistically warm my core.

53 Whenever we create or support an evil entity to combat an evil entity, we always end up with an evil entity.

54 When I told my wife I needed to lose a lot more stomach to get better core rotation in the surfski, she lovingly told me I might have to "learn to be hungry!" She's right; now I'm sad!

55 Once is bad; twice is really bad, and more than twice qualifies as a serial offender and possibly incorrigible.

56 My wife and I both like when I'm not hardheaded about my being hardheaded.

57 I love staring into shallow, clear water, but it breaks my heart I can't often kayak in it.

58 The only thing possibly more pathetic and tragic than lusting after thoughts or things in the future is lusting after memories of things that were or weren't.

59 All I ever wanted to be was raw bone; all I got was raw.

60 Sadly, my overt failures and feelings of worthlessness associated with the remembrance of them work against my wanting to be successful in almost any endeavor.

61 The preponderance of my ugly behavior over the years has always been rooted in deep-seated insecurities.

62 Best not tarry when distributaries become tributaries.

63 I am monogamous in marriage but rather polyamorous when it comes to surfskis.

64 The meaning of "this is not Disney" has done a 180 over the last few sunlit years.

65 "Strange" will trap a fella every time; strange water will free a paddler most of the time.

66 Lazy and self-centeredness have a very recognizable and similar genome.

67 If it's antithetical to the Gospel, then it will eventually not be peaceful.

68 Brevity matters.

69   Too much information and inflammation are kinfolks.

70   Neither mustard nor pumpkin orange are real good colors for fat folks.

71   God says He always was; I believe it, but I sure can't comprehend "always was."

72   If the debt doesn't get us, the "vig" surely will.

73   Regarding physicality: I have to often remind my addict self that I don't have to kayak the entire lake today; I just need to kayak.

74   Though still way beyond my intellect, I am better able to comprehend and be at peace with Eternity existing in the future elsewhere than on this sin-ravaged planet.

75   When I don't feel like doing it right now, I probably should do it right now.

76   Every day paddling is either good for me, even if not good to me; or, good to me, even if not good for me.

77   Working on an advanced degree and being in the military have the following in common: they both include following directions, being clear and concise in communication, and learning time-tested procedures.

78   Invidious invincibility creates hegemony.

79   Overachieving is exhausting, so I've been told.

80   "Thankful" is a complete thought whether imperative, interrogative, exclamatory, or declarative; however, it is best when not conditional.

81   Some cans of worms spread germs, and it might be better to leave them unopened, particularly when going fishing.

82. Rebellion lay upon the shoulders of the rebellious, but there are unseen marionette masters very adept at inciting it.

83. As someone who has never truly been hungry, I am completely incapable of judging the behavior of castaways trying to survive.

84. When I am often reminded there are children and women all over the world being trafficked and abused, it makes it difficult to hold on to hope for humanity…only God…

85. Burning bridges has consequences, but some bridges are toxic.

86. It's human nature to lash out; it's God's nature not to.

87. I believe some men get into yoga initially not because of the increased flexibility and overall sense of well-being but because they heard there was a position called the downward dog.

Chapter 28

1. I remember when substances, which made me high, led to sleep where nothingness was like being high, because nothingness feels nothing.

2. We are a quick-fix generation.

3. Being the toughest guy at a frat party doesn't carry much weight in the Hoosegow.

4. We are awake for a reason.

5. Awake and woke are not synonymous in the 21st Century.

6. When and if the young guys beat the old guys, it's often because the old guys taught the young guys their tricks and skills.

7. Sorry! No offense intended, but if you send it and whatever it is exceeds five minutes, there is a solid chance I am not going to watch it, unless it involves kayaks or surfskis.

8. Give me a little Wisdom and I'll quickly and tragically turn it into pride.

9. Addicts rarely measure.

10. The fat may be in and on my body, but it started in my head.

11. As an addict, I tend toward excess; however, to celebrate excess is shameful.

12. If you helped me and I don't give you public attribution, it is likely because I figured you may not want credit for what I perceive as improvement.

13   J. Edgar Hoover's maxim "you either improve or deteriorate" does not put me in good stead.

14   There are few folks who work as hard as a committed, recovering addict working crappy jobs while endeavoring to get his or her life back in order.

15   I'm serious when I say it is serious when serious folks don't take serious things seriously.

16   I can't buy back, borrow, or steal a day I didn't paddle.

17   Hard to put a premium on coaches who know their stuff, practice what they preach, and are vested in helping their athletes, clients, and protegees.

18   In my case, technique is painstakingly learned, not inherent.

19   The insatiably curious often find out their shoe size the hard way.

20   So much of what we believe is justified by what we believe.

21   Though a thankful product of Manifest Destiny, I am no longer an adherent.

22   Sometimes, too much still is not enough.

23   It's hard to throw away what I'll never use.

24   Knowing more than someone does not necessarily make one wiser.

25   Bureaucrats fear entrepreneurs.

26   The greatest con I ever tried to pull and sadly still do, is thinking I am conning God.

27 One of the most overused, often erroneous statements, in this age of non-responsibility is: "I know my boy couldn't have done it; he's a good boy!"

28 Flesh and blood matter, but they are not the end-all.

29 Because God "never satisfies the cravings of the wicked," they never stop craving.

30 I pray not for wealth, but for my children to have God's favor, and that He may grant my wife and me many more years of healthy living.

31 I'm like a lot of redeemed folks with scar tissue--I have good days and difficult days.

32 Kuki Gallmann Dreamed of Africa; I just dream of water, whether awake or asleep.

33 The phrase, "There is not a Mensa among 'em," merely acknowledges that Houston might have a problem.

34 Just because I too often wear my emotions on my sleeves doesn't mean I enjoy it or approve the message.

35 We are all Pygmalion proteges in God's economy.

36 Pulpeteering that doesn't include the "hard things" is suspect.

37 If it's "just fluid," it still qualifies as weight.

38 False teachings muddy the water of Truth.

39 I know a rich man who once taught me about obligation; then, over time, his wealth and the power he wielded with it seemingly caused him to forget all he ever taught me.

40   In America, it's not uncommon for the haves and have-nots to struggle financially less than the sorta-haves—fortune does not always favor the middle class.

41   War, any war, is a tragic way to check Malthusian determinism.

42   Resentments blind us to Truth.

43   The thin line between dirty and necessary is but a tattered silk thread.

44   While not a proponent of the Great Man Theory, every successful team endeavor requires a strong leader.

45   Some folks with little feet sure have a big footprint.

46   It is not always easy being easy.

47   I may not want for anything more, but sadly still likely want for more.

48   Politics is a piss-poor programmatic process for progress.

49   Only fools or institutions full of fools could possibly think or justify spending more than they take in and expect to be solvent.

50   There are times when the only choice is not a choice.

51   The best way to tell the Truth is to tell the truth.

52   I don't want to be an influencer; I just want to influence.

53   The color of colors changes due to perception.

54   Soldiering, policing, and politicking may mix, but they don't mix well.

55   Life is simpler when we keep it simple.

56 Misty water-colored memories of the way things were or could have been can drown a fella if he lets 'em.

57 Some folks think the devil is just ridin', but he has likely been drivin' all along; his name is on the pink slip.

58 I may not always understand Him, but God always knows what He's doing.

59 We are never too far-gone, unless we are too far-gone.

60 I may think I know, but I really don't.

61 Many of us who "deal with stuff" have survived periodic seasons of squalor.

62 If I want to be the recipient of allowances for when I have bad days, then I need to make allowances for others having a bad day.

63 Today, the sun finally set on cool! Rest in Peace, Red Paden! I love you!

64 New habits often portend new beginnings.

65 I often cringe at the thought of things that I thought mattered.

66 Scum congregates.

67 Thank-you notes are like TripAdvisor reviews, if you don't write them within 24 hours, then it likely is not going to happen.

68 Old can be older than older, and older can be older than old; yet, oldest is older than both.

69 When my illusions become delusions, they are sadly paired with grandeur.

70 If Job had to put a hand over his mouth after being admonished by the Lord for his foolish understanding, then Ole Malachi doesn't have enough hands.

71 The depth of a relationship is often attributed to the rubs having been worked through and forgiven.

72 Playing a rube is easier if you don't have to play.

73 Agitators and political bloviators are often one and the same.

74 I have finally, over time, realized wealth is not what I thought it was.

75 When I trust folks, I don't really know with my thoughts, it's often because I think too highly of myself and my flawed perception that they feel the same way about me.

76 Truth doesn't live in a vacuum or a petri dish.

77 "We have all sinned and fallen short of the Glory of God," is a true statement when used generally as an apology for a specific slight; yet, it is a very poor amend.

78 The right words are a wooer.

79 More finite is not necessarily an oxymoron.

80 I am more fragile than I realize; I am stronger than I realize.

81 Aaah, to be a crofter in Scotland.

82 Largely, we have become inured in the 1st world to the daily miraculous.

83 Beware the honey pot, for it is not.

84 Just because someone pays me for a service I provide does not mean he or she can dictate how I provide it, particularly if it is not within the parameters of what I advertise, communicate, and offer.

85 Preternatural curiosity can lead to fathomless, dysphoric darkness if left unchecked.

86 Check a fool, and he is going to act a fool.

87 Palpable angst should lead to empathy.

88 Some folks love quotas until quotas affect service.

89 I should better heed the first rumblings of impatience.

90 When the 3:00 a.m. voice harangues me with bad memories and peccadilloes that I know have been forgiven, it is not God's voice.

91 The Trojan horse did not stay in Troy; it is among us.

92 As long as I don't drag the past or the future into the present, then the present stays present, as do I.

Chapter 29

1. The beginning of wisdom often begins with our first concrete realization that we are not "all that!"

2. When prosecuting becomes persecuting, things are not copacetic.

3. Historically, swords for hire have never worked well for the home team.

4. I don't like to hear what I don't want to hear, but I often need to hear what I don't want to hear.

5. Sophistic sensibilities rest near the heart of deceit.

6. When every man is no longer a soldier, society may be temporarily at peace, but it is likely soft.

7. "Spiritually certain" need not be uncertain, but periodic testing is healthy.

8. German efficiency and Swiss precision are non-sequiturs in the Mississippi Delta, but I love her nonetheless.

9. The longer I live, the less credit I can take for knowing God.

10. Little scratches my fiber like a person of Faith who expects or demands a discount due to being a person of Faith.

11. The obviously fictitious arguments I have with people in my head that never materialize are legion.

12. To have a life partner—wife, lover, friend, muse—with whom I can comfortably and safely discuss things that matter and things that don't is one of God's richest blessings! I am blessed far beyond desert.

13. One upside to the Covid-era run on toilet paper was that the hoarder's excess may have finally been put to good use for those unaccustomed to its liberal use.

14. I am an "immerser" who prefers brief forays.

15. What's behind me is not important unless it's about to catch me.

16. God will act when He acts.

17. When a people tell you, "it's not my business," then get in your business, obviously they think it is their business.

18. When injured or sad, I go into a remote place and "lick my wounds." When Jesus was sad over cousin John's death, he went to a remote place and licked all the wounds of those who followed him.

19. If I pray for God's will, then finagle stuff to make it work, then it probably is not His will and likely won't work.

20. Sadly, I may be a bit of a cynic, but swimming out to meet every troop ship can have adverse effects on the economy and psyche!

21. I'm as open of a book as I'm willing to open.

22. "We are chosen, yet we choose,"—in my limited understanding—is where Calvin and Arminius meet; beyond that, pedantic semantics likely ensues.

23. I used to really think voting made a difference.

24. I firmly believe that , on the whole, our two-party system is nothing more than a touch football game between skins and shirts: the parties don't care which side they're on as long as they get to play and we get tackled. It's all a show.

25 The Mississippi Delta in winter is no longer verdant; it looks like Harvey Updyke has been around with some glyphosate, but there is still a beautiful alienation.

26 Smart people listen.

27 Working does not automatically equate to working class, and working class does not necessarily imply working.

28 Health and right thinking are connected.

29 God's economy is not our economy.

30 Fog can be instructive.

31 Forgiveness is important for any offense, but it is more easily bestowed if asked for specifically.

32 The very occasional joke or funny meme is tolerable; constant clowning exhausts me.

33 The value of some things tossed is all in how they're tossed.

34 What appears to a constant paddler to be ripples from the shoreline is usually waves in the middle.

35 The "Trojan Horse" is not just a myth. It's alive, well, and belly full; and, I may be it.

36 The ignorance of the ignorant is evidenced when we mock what we don't understand.

37 The pleasures of sin are as fleeting as the wind; one is left with exhaustion and shame.

38 Acting ugly takes a lot out of me.

39 I'm fairly adept at disposing disposable income.

40 The liminal quintessence of the Mississippi Delta is not easily defined.

41 Memory Lane has no forward gear.

42 My largely unrecognized, never expressed nor formulated, definitely unrequited goal in life is to be an exceptional everyman, only if…

43 Get conned by enough carpetbaggers and scalawags even the village idiot becomes cynical.

44 We can admire someone's resiliency without admiring the person's character.

45 The real beauty of a church should not be the edifice.

46 Almost five and a half years in Recovery and I am finally beginning to understand the way to be good to myself is to not do things that bring temporal pleasures that are not good for me.

47 Greatest line, by a confidential informant, on Chicago PD in eleven seasons, "It's Chicago, bribe someone!"

48 I hurt when I kayak; I hurt when I don't; I'd rather hurt when I do!

49 I need to be concerned with doing right for right's sake more than for doing right for image sake.

50 Figure out the source of animal instinct and one might be halfway to Heaven.

51 In the Mississippi Delta, we might not know what savoir-faire is, but we do know just what to do in any given situation.

52 Most "money-back guarantees" guarantee we are going to swim against a riptide to get our money back.

53 When my past taunts me and haunts me in the witching hour like a wide-eyed owl on its nightly prowl, I finally say, "Get behind me," with God's help.

54 Sadly, there are many things I largely quit caring about a long time ago, not because they are unimportant, but due to their appearing solution-less, except to politicians in an election season.

55 Back doors are commonsensical except for addicts.

56 I try to stay just enough aware that I'm aware, but not so aware of things I can't control that I stay anxious and depressed.

57 In America today, those who proclaim to be "in the middle" do not revere the middle class.

58 Not relaxing, makes swallowing any pill--physical or metaphorical--difficult.

59 I'm heterosexual, but I do love a good show tune.

60 The most conspicuous variable in any situation is usually the self.

61 So much of what we love and value in life is often more about a shared experience than the experience itself.

62 I'm too old and set in my ways to swim out to meet troop ships; they've got to find me if they want my delicacies.

63 I am thankful for a wife who doesn't react to my reactions, thereby nullifying a chain reaction.

64 Qualitative has more to do with feeling and perception than fact.

65 Redemption is not, nor should be, static or a one-off.

66 For those who think telling lies can produce favorable outcomes need heed the proverb, "Telling lies about others is as harmful as hitting them with an ax."

67 Instead of quelling riots, we are afraid of riots, thereby condoning them.

68 The presence of leaders who uncover the "deeds of the foul" causes the demons to scream.

69 An upside to being an addict/alcoholic is that due to our excess, if we recognize it because of the effects of excess, we seek help.

70 Listening to Glenn Campbell on the road reminds me of delightful moments in the barber shop as a child in the 60s and 70s reading Field and Stream right before Daddy had the barber skin my head like a Comanche war party.

71 My wife saw goodness in me when I wasn't sure there was any left.

72 Balancing the buzz was a very difficult element of active addiction; at times, I do miss the buzz, but definitely not the balancing or the after effect.

73 Obsessive-compulsiveness and perfectionism are not synonymous.

74 Amazing what I have proclaimed as fact over the years simply because I was told it was fact.

75 Idols and icons have a lot in common.

76 The "blind" perceive not the Darkness.

77 It is eminently possible to admire many of someone's qualities while fearing them as a person.

78 I need to do what I need to do when I need to do it, or I don't do it.

79   The rube is not always a rube.

80   Compensatory facades are rarely compensatory.

81   When folks are repeatedly told what doesn't belong to them belongs to them, then they are apt to take what doesn't belong to them.

82   Liminal junctures between land and water are never fully static.

83   One cannot acclimate to rough waters without spending time in rough waters.

84   Marriage used to be a thing.

85   Over the last few years of being clean and sober, this addict has finally found enjoyment in even one thin mint; however, I'd still prefer 20!

86   Oh, that my heart's cry for the needs of others would be that of Jesus: "I am willing!"

87   Words influence; actions solidify.

88   Judas is not just among us; he is we.

89   Tragic how often I willingly or unwittingly pocket 30 pieces of silver.

Chapter 30

1. Learned behavior can be unlearned; it just is not easy.

2. Immediacy can be debilitating.

3. If everything affects me, then less of everything is still a lot more than nothing.

4. Nothingness shadows evil, and evil veils nothingness, while "not-nothingness" is a manifestation of something more than nothing.

5. If it's not more, but it's right, then it is not less.

6. Social media has made me think my voice is bigger than it is and bigger than it should be.

7. If we are not thankful, then we are not rooted.

8. My old-age mantra: consume less, waste less, litter not.

9. When I "get to eating," I sure stretch a lot quicker than a tree trunk.

10. Even the thought of happy times makes me sad.

11. I am growing weary due to modernity.

12. I never cease to be amazed at how ignorant some truly gifted people can be.

13. One can be low maintenance and "to-the-manner born."

14. Some folks would have an easier time spotting a camouflaged copperhead among dry leaves than the Truth.

15. Some folks don't even realize they snarl.

16 Semi-allegiances are hard to maintain.

17 Alcohol and drugs do not create dishonesty; they merely bring it out and exacerbate it.

18 Amazing how my twenty years Out West is encapsulated into, "Yes, I spent about twenty years out West!"

19 I finally like being me.

20 Many intuitive people still swim around in a fish bowl.

21 I've spent most of my life either making amends or making messes that need amends.

22 I even feel guilty scattering buzzards off roadkill.

23 I rarely see a body of water where I don't want to kayak.

24 A dead bovine is a Brazilian Steakhouse for buzzards.

25 In today's economy, pets often mean more, because people mean less.

26 I fear I post on Social Media too often for the sad sake of relevance.

27 Sometimes, that "heard stuff" is scarier than that "saw stuff."

28 For one who gets bored with the status quo, I sure don't like change.

29 "She's had some work done" no longer refers to the home.

30 Too many folks can always find a reason not to tip a servant.

31 When on the water or on the road, I prefer to have the environment set the mood rather than music; it's more natural and less overstimulating.

32 Accolades are for the living.

33 An "Army of One" is an oxymoron, unless you're Chuck Norris.

34 If you have a million questions, I don't have a million answers.

35 I fail to find any Rothchilds, Rockefellers, or "rock stars" on the front lines of any intended or actual wars.

36 Determinism is no justification for most of what passes for social justice today.

37 In my world, one sip is not a slip; it's a fall from Grace.

38 I need to do what I know to do when I know to do what I need to do.

39 I crave pleasure because my mind tricks me into thinking it will make me feel better. I do finally understand why, but it still leaves me sad.

40 The flat lands are my home.

41 I read and listen to Proverbs but not sure I really listen and do…

42 If I'm found to be humorless because I find no humor in taking God's name in vain or for making light of his name or purposes, then, so be it.

43 How one views a landlord depends on whether he is one or is a renter.

44 The lion's share of my stupid stuff has been committed when broken and lonely or self-imposed on a mountaintop.

45 The more we are at the mercy of government, the less we receive mercy.

46 Bullets cannot pierce angel skins.

47 Alienation is often more prevalent in the busiest of places.

48   I likely will agree more with a rabid conservative than a thoughtful liberal, but I would likely rather have a dialogue with a thoughtful liberal than a rabid conservative: thoughtful and rabid being operative words.

49   My wife is a free spirit; I just have a spirit yearning to be free.

50   I often miss the childhood I took for granted.

51   Authentic people don't want "watered-down" anything.

52   Unrestrained hegemony propagated by un-elected power brokers will place the last straw on the camel's back of any Republic.

53   One cannot just tell a dog or a child, who is involuntarily shaking due to abject fear—warranted or not—to just stop shaking; however, they can be comforted, which is likely to mitigate it.

54   I'm much more comfortable talking about how sorry I was and am than I am trying to hide or defend how sorry I was and am.

55   Memory Lane has more briars than I anticipated.

56   There's a lot more truth evident in older cop shows.

57   Back in time, time wasn't always kind.

58   I find myself watching old cop shows to avoid the constructed non-reality of "liquid modernity."

59   Imaginary arguments can consume an addict.

60   Complicated becomes simple when society collapses.

61   To judge based on flawed, not-investigated presuppositions is the height of ignorance.

62   Grace plus choice consummate life.

63 Justice has no middle ground.

64 My "exploration" phase started later and lasted longer than most folks.

65 Some things named New Life are not.

66 My wife graciously allows me to be a poor philosopher.

67 My hypocrisy may not bother me as much as yours does, but it should.

68 It's hard to see and hear the Truth through clutter.

69 I don't feed, fight, or fool with trolls.

70 The concern with Leviathan is in its nature and its size; the bigger it gets, the more it wants.

71 As a rule, the richer you are, the better you're treated, until a revolution comes.

72 Social media creates too many comparisons between people and things.

73 Dead religion produces death.

74 "They" don't have to understand our choices; only we and God do.

75 Age and life have ameliorated my iconoclasm.

76 The closer my Faith mirrors my Recovery and the closer my Recovery mirrors my Faith the healthier I am.

77 Confidence is best served when rooted in pleasing God and not worrying what others think about us, if our behavior is pleasing to God.

78 Hegemony could easily be spelled like it could phonetically be spelled: "hedge money."

79 A basic or even deeper understanding of systematic theology does not automatically equate or lead to practice or a life well-lived and pleasing to God.

80 It's hard being mean and sensitive.

81 Spiritually, I crave authenticity within order. I refer to it as "Chestertonian orthodoxy."

82 God is reason, non-reason, and far exalted above both.

83 The conspiracy is often the cover-up.

84 The devil loves division, and social media is his sword.

85 The majority supporting what is right is not evidence of what is right, but likely evidence that what is right has influenced the majority.

86 It's not that I don't want one, I just can't stop at one; and, even if I could stop at one, I would still want one more; and the wanting can be almost as detrimental to my mentality as having one more.

87 Liberal sensibilities are not antithetical to orthodox conservatism.

Chapter 31

1 Absolutes are absolutely absolute.

2 Gratitude is great; gratitude shared is greater.

3 God's sovereignty is the source of Grace.

4 It's a frightful thing to guard the righteous.

5 To those who thought that I thought that I was better than they were, whether or not I did or didn't, I have proven them to be wrong.

6 It's difficult for an addict to eat less than the "whole enchilada."

7 Exaggerations have a tendency to negate the point.

8 Often, the checking of one's own people evidences the strength in one's convictions.

9 I love quotes, but I'm tired of slogans.

10 When we die, it's all over…down here.

11 At times, I think folks think I'm smarter than I am, when they likely think I'm not as smart as I think I am.

12 Opportunity costs cost, but meditating on them after the fact costs more.

13 People notice punctuation, even if they don't use it often.

14 For the broken-hearted, good memories can be much more deleterious to the psyche than painful ones.

15 Excess is exhausting.

16   The biggest sense of gravity in a Christian's life is the downward pull of the world.

17   If I would hesitate to broach it with you in person, I sure shouldn't broach it on social media.

18   I never knew I was an addict until I knew I was an addict.

19   The more of the world I see, the harder it is to see it.

20   It's best for a non-sausage maker not to comment on sausage making during the process.

21   If we narrow our search for the Truth, it can be hard to find.

22   Never judge another fella by your definition of cool.

23   I can't always say I am doing something because I'm not him, but maybe, doing it because I just don't want to be like him.

24   I didn't hear actual voices in my head, but the non-voice voices in my head influenced me in active addiction.

25   It's hard to be Holy at the beach.

26   Recovery, life, and God's Word have taught me to be careful with saying "never," but to say God willing and "One Day at a Time."

27   Walls inherently imply something within is worth protecting.

28   If we think we are better than we are, then we will not try to be better than we are, which means we aren't as good as we think we are!

29   Being kind and nice regardless of the situation is much easier on the sensitive in the long run.

30   Little improves one's character and reputation more than death.

31 The dissolution of love is life's greatest tragedy.

32 As an old man, I now view Dylan Thomas's admonitions differently.

33 We may not recognize the crossroads because we may already be in it.

34 We seem to admire most those who never forget where they came from.

35 Truth need not be compromised, but the application of it can be a result of a compromise.

36 God sees behind the mask and the curtain.

37 Even a TV death affects me.

38 Remove the source of the cravings-psychological or physical—and the cravings are mitigated.

39 The foolishness of mankind is evidenced in our too-oft willingness to throw "everything that matters away" for a moment of pleasure, even when we know better.

40 I struggle with the intersection of the past and the future at the Crossroads of the present.

41 When "the rubber meets the road" the rubber is spinning and the road, reality, is in a state of inertia.

42 I fear I too often couch and justify my sins and weaknesses behind the veil of my just being sensitive.

43 I don't even know what alright is, but I'm okay today.

44 Being sensitive is painful.

45 I live between Harry Chapin's Verities and Balderdash, 'tween the Cradle and the Crown.

46   Just because I'm somnolent doesn't mean I sleep too much.

47   Even 50 years later, the high school pecking order is hard to shake.

48   Living the Gospel is presenting the Gospel.

49   My metro-redneck sensibilities are best evidenced by my excitement when Val Kilmer's Doc Holiday puts lead in Johnny Ringo's forehead and my tearful reaction when Bingley proposes to Jane, Darcy proposes to Elizabeth, Hugh Grant's Edward proposes to Elinor Dashwood, and when Madge tells me she loves and admires me!

50   The size of a fish only matters after the first one.

51   Dixie need not be a pejorative.

52   Good memories truly can be the most painful, because the events creating them didn't last.

53   When I see or think about all the lonely people, I have a hard time swallowing.

54   I emote though rarely rote.

55   There is no judgment when you Hill Country Blues shuffle.

56   I hate when I get rid of things I need—when I get rid of things I need.

57   It's hard to bootstrap when one has no boots.

58   As if reality isn't skewed enough, along comes AI.

59   The story of mankind makes no sense without God, the Creator.

60   Pulling together the content of a book seems to require more than a thousand cuts, dices, and slices.

⁶¹   I don't like chatter when trying to listen or think.

⁶²   How easily the ignorant, without invitation, touch another person's horse, motorcycle, wheelchair, and loved one.

⁶³   I daily pray for Wisdom to help me in my ignorance; and, as Wisdom intervenes, the better I realize my ignorance.

⁶⁴   Social media posts, even pithy ones, are the antithesis of a slow-burning flame. The flash is blinding, even amazing, then it's gone.

⁶⁵   I pray our forthcoming book, "Wrestling with Wisdom at the Crossroads," will honor God, and if it honors Him, He will do with it as He pleases.

⁶⁶   What I too often consider as human frailties in my life are also too often really sins against God as I go my own way.

⁶⁷   When life chips away at arrogance, humility is a much better option than resentment.

⁶⁸   I used to lose things I misplaced, now I lose things I'm looking at.

⁶⁹   I desire to release all that binds me and to bind all that binds me.

⁷⁰   I need to pray for myself what I pray for others; I need to pray for others what I pray for myself.

⁷¹   I'm bad about saying the blessing before a meal with the fork already in my hand, "my mind on my meal and my meal on my mind."

⁷²   A man with a whole lot of money, a shallow internal compass, and an unchecked libido is potentially a very dangerous man.

⁷³   Life-past boils down like bone broth to an obituary, at best.

74   Social Media and Internet news inject too much foreign, electronic DNA into my simple strain of Southern agrarian living. It changes who I am and who I'm meant to be.

75   Double-blade paddling, side-to-side, like a metronome, is the rhythm of my life.

76   We are not our best selves by ourselves.

77   Most of us, even if not country music fans, want at some point in our complicated life, to go to Luckenbach, Texas.

78   Those who hurt when loved ones have been hurt often remember the hurt better than those being hurt.

79   Some wounds are just too deep not to cauterize.

80   Poetry is easier than politics, a heck of a lot more enjoyable, though just as confusing, and does not provoke vomitus eruptus.

81   I'm a troubadour who can't carry a tune nor light up a room, yet I write and think...

82   I don't have a hard time "releasing" resentments; I'm just bad about picking them back up.

83   All of my life, God has mercifully kept a veil over what I was about to see.

84   The more I stretch, the looser I get; the looser I get, the more I stretch.

85   I don't take bad news well, nor am I appropriately thankful for good news.

86   Everybody has his or her own walk, and they don't need the burden of my resentments, which are really my burden.

87 If I am affected by everything I watch, then I need to quit watching everything that affects me.

88 Praying does not make us bulletproof, but likely spares us legions of unseen ammo.

89 Wrestling with Wisdom is a cage match between good and evil.

POEMS

...without a hurt the heart is hollow.

— EL GALLO, "THE FANTASTICKS"

Soul of the Poet

Soul of the poet
frought with pain
soul of the poet
outside the main
the poet's soul
knows no bounds
feet firmly off the ground
head in the heavens
heart in the breech
searching for reason
purpose and reach
paths unpredicted
austere, forlorn
foot before the other
tattered with scorn
visage shattered
emotions in tatters
pores secreting
all that matters
yearning for answers
none rarely given
highway detritus
leaving him shriven
affected by all
all not resolved
piercing the gloaming
a siren's call
shipwreck presaged
determinism set
free will an option
magnetic the net
melodies warble
dragnet complete
resistance futile
a Faustian meet

the poet may wander
windmills to tilt
Pilgrim's Progress
relieving the guilt
path not known
the poet may groan
onward he stumbles
drawn the unknown
sirens may shriek
compelled he may be
listen for whispers
God he may meet
nerves red with raw
rationalists guffaw
straggle he may
searching the way
crossroads before him
SEEK THE WAY!

The Elephant's Graveyard

A poem written in three stages over a month that included pre, during and post Recovery under the nom de plume, Slim Gravy.

APRIL 2018

I flew too close to the sun today. Sometimes things just work out
    that way.

When wings are spread, neck craned and winter's dormancy sheds its
    mane, spring burgeons brightly rending hibernation's complacency.

New growth bursts forth, pains of labor shattering winter's easy dealings
    as longer days thin blood amidst spring's warm awakening!

Life renews! Hope restored! Healthy things grow! But, it ain' always easy!

I live in the elephant's graveyard, where the sun seems to always shine,
    where clouds appear as grey memories, flitting across the landscape,
    littered with bleached bones, plucked clean of all the mean!

EARLY SEPT

I slowly sink toward unknown depths, air hard to find in the stifling
    mire, no gills, chest about to burst, heavy-laden with liquid sacs of
    cerise sorrow...

EARLY OCTOBER

In-treatment the cure, dark roads turned brilliant, vulnerability the key,
    petitions answered promptly, Him who is able answers timely,
    friends and family my juggernaut, hope restored, sins forgiven,
    diseases healed, extraction from the pit, love and compassion
    crowned, restoration imminent and ongoing; God be thanked!

Precarious the Sanity of He Who Walks Alone

An addict Reflects on Donne:

    Precarious the sanity of he who walks alone
    Fiery barbs piercing 'neath the loam
    Vile thoughts incarnate
    Spiking membrane's sheath
    A faith-filled shield the only
    Phylactery revealed
    To rebuff the Foul ones lust
    In pursuit of Hade's nil.
    No man an island
    Donne did utter
    Singular promontories
    Cascading to the sea
    Continents no longer static
    Transformed with ev'ry slide
    Pieces chiseled from the whole
    Isolation bereft of Hope
    Thoughts sequestered bound within
    God alone can change the tone
    Of the recluse's anthem
    The piper piped his lyrical lies
    Contrived to lead astray

His breath so foul
His visage scowled
Beneath the angel's light
True self revealed
When mankind heels
Obeying what not he knows
We need God
And one another
A true friend sits
For a brother
Solitude we need
But best to heed
And never schlepp alone…
Yes, never schlepp alone…

Disease of More

Disease of More
Is not just lore—
Cunning, baffling, conniving

Conspires against
Those on the fence
Marauding all that's Holy

It wants it all
It heeds the call
From none but the unholy

This unknown cure
Engulfs the pure
Wasting all that surrounds it

It cries, "More, More,"
It keeps close score
And always wins the battle

We must not yield
The playing field
To what seeks our destruction

The leech cried, "Give,
Succumb and live,"
Knowing too well our weakness

Deny ourselves
What's on the shelves
Or we shall surely falter

If we look high
'Tween land and sky
We might avoid destruction.

For this:

Disease of More
Is not just lore—
Cunning, baffling, conniving.

Eye to Eye

Eye to eye
Speaks the lie
Confounded in the orb

Motives hid
'Hind the lid
Twinkles diffusing Truth

Nods and winks
Make one think
Veracity aloof

Route to soul
Sayings old
Yet proven over time

Eye doth hold
Tears so bold
In silence it does speak

Wet or dry
Foul the lie
Reflections in design

Stink eye mean
Red eye lean
Yet clear eye seen serene

Eyes with tells
Sound the bells
They're tolling just for thee

Raven's peck
Dealer's deck
They tell what tells do tell

Hearts deemed pure
Hold allure
As seen through God's own eyes

Do not lie
Cleanse the eye
So others can see God

Splendor reigns
Red the veins
Of he who toes the line

We can't hide
Nor abide
A fabricator's truth

Truth it ain'
Lies be taint
Fidelity desired

Eyes inform
Hidden norms
Patterns not oft displayed

Poe did know
Eyes do show
The hidden tell-tale heart…

Lord, cleanse my lens, Please!

Consumed by Him the Addict

A time to think
A time to drink
Better to seek the prior
Combustion said
Goes to the head
Of the seeking outlier
Outcroppings draw
The screeching maw
'Scaping the widow's pyre
Her bread is gone
Her lot forlorn
Why did he choose the latter?
The widow's mite
Has little fight
When her covering is gone
The addict's breath
Sadly bereft
For concern beyond himself
He meant no harm
Too long the arm
Reaching for what is folly
Some hold it well
Some heed the swell
Of that which would capsize 'em

Underlings die
When raw the rye
Consumed by him the addict
The widow may
Still save the day
By calling upon the Lord
Our only hope
How long the rope
From His hands unto ours
As long as is
As long as His
Eternity before us
We need but heed
The broken reed
Of One who still confines us
He'll never bruise
He'll never ruse
The tender ones who seek Him
The addict and
His widow's hand
Are never beyond His reach
But both must strive
To stay alive
Relinquishing all to Him
The addict may
Still be okay
If he will just surrender
The addict may
Not have his way
If he is to surrender…

∾

At Our Creator's Beckon

West 'cross the bay
Doth Gatsby pray
Beseeching summer solstice
Winter's moon
Cries loud the loon
Turn just a wee bit faster
Water breathes
Noxious reprieves
Brume emerging gently
Zephyr still
'Gainst Neptune's will
Jupiter stays silent
Returns the breeze
Heard 'mongst the trees
Shrouding cypress shore line
Tupelos bend
When starts the wind
Their seeds anxious to wander
Young the night
Preceding light
When Pluto seeks his harvest
If Saturn's seed
Will not concede
Groundhog's shadow lengthens
Yet...spring will rise
'Neath the skies
At our Creator's beckon.

Being Southern

The first one said
Messed with my head
I'm inherently lazy

She may be right
And what a fright
For one who's toiled all his life

My idle comes
Not from being a bum
But just from being Southern

We till the land
Eschew the Man
And value time reflecting

We chew and shoot
Don't give a hoot
'Bout things that don't concern us

Oh, grouse we might
But in the light
Where hidden things don't prosper

Not too afraid
Stoic and staid
Wanton in our excesses

To understand
The Southern Man
It takes more than a minute

We want it all
Our siren's call
It doth surely define us

WRESTLING WITH WISDOM AT THE CROSSROADS

Randy and coy
Our Mama's boy
Yet rife with vim and venom

We'll scratch for cat
Yet pass the hat
For loved ones and the stranger

Complex we are
Feathers and tar
Augment our understanding

God and soldier
Make us bolder
Much better than we are

For kith and kin
We'll commit sin
Though we do know the better

Staunch on fight day
We'll hold the sway
For what we see is right

But sans the fight
It jus' ain' right
To avoid contemplation

So when you fear
A Rebel's cheer
Thank God that we're amongst you!

Being Southern ain' a sin. It's a calling!

God Showed Me Many Mountains

God showed me many mountains,
oceans deep and blue,
and every single forest,
verdant, lush and true

True to primal intentions,
pristine, orderly and pure,
only man hath desecrated,
that made to endure

Endure for many ages,
until complete His plans,
redeeming all the faithful,
a new world in His hands

Hands scarred and weary,
ears tired from all the noise,
reducing contemplation,
eroding Peace and joy

Joy overshadowed,
by over-stimulation,
speakers blaring loudly,
destroying pontification

Pontification matters,
must reflect and think,
without this prime indulgence,
mankind at the brink

The brink where all the lemmings,
rush wildly to the sea,
not stopping at cliff's edge,
auguring misery

Misery antithetical,
to a thankful heart,
God will show us much,
if we'll just do our part

The part that really matters,
beckons us to bend,
the knee in genuflection,
then hearts begin to mend

Mending tortured souls,
and we mending our ways,
helps us make amends,
fueling peace-filled days

Days surely numbered,
no one knows the hour,
when tolls the bell at day's end,
our last breath as a flower

The flower with all its allure,
surely fades in just a day,
yet God brandished His splendor,
time to seize the day—Carpe diem.

Things Done and Left Undone

Things done and left undone
Would be my undoing
If not for the Grace of God
I would lie in ruin

To be forgiven, due to Love
Love, not of my doing
Freely, yet costly, given
Redeeming my undoing

To lose the weight and lightly walk
Into Life illuminated
I shed my sin, begin again
Life anew, 'til again I sin

Yet, when I sin once again
Vicariously benefitting from
What God, Himself, wrought in blood
Undoing what I have done.

~

Eternity Stranded in Time

Dedicated to Michael Card, whose reverent theology, fathomless insight, musical skill set, and Christ-centered anthologies have changed my life.

Eternity, stranded in time
is not an easy get
a paradox explaining the
Forever of our soul.
Our mortal coil shall soon divest
and shed its carbon husk
retaining only spirit, the body revolved to dust.
Dust to dust and sin to sin
forgiveness sought in the end.
Eternity will be, is and was
a concept beyond compare.
The Ancient of Days always was
He's ever been right here.
How could a Being always be
and never was not was.
This alone demands a search
Eternity never bound
by false constraints
nor man's complaints
seek Him while He'll be found.
Eternity, stranded in time
is truly here and now
yet, when we die tis no lie
Eternity found unbound.

~

Ode to a Fallen Kokopelli

My heart is sheered
A sentinel shattered
Oh Watcher of the Wake
Why have you fallen?
How long you stood
Genuflected and bent
Eyeing your charges
Guarding their tombs
A "type of Christ"
A seer most revered
Protecting the interred
Shepherding thy realm
Hallowed ground you nurtured
Nourished by the same
Never your post abandoned
Never a complaint
It took a mighty sheer wind
To shake your stalwart core
Roots aged and haggard
Yielding 'neath the blow
Your purpose now is served
Noble sentry now deceased
You leave a sylvan vacuum
Requiescet in pace—Peace

Sin Whispers to Evil

Sin Whispers to Evil
with foul intent
mayhem a gown
hegemony uncloaked
chaos unfettered
milk for the simple
wine for the dying
oxygen for the frail
bedlam unfettered
fear beyond the pale
hatred and malice
heart's effluence toxic
the devil's lair
sires division
disseverance propagates
emitting pernicious odors
masked not by roses
nor occluded by pretension
one atom of excreta
taints the whole bouquet
as one ray of light
dispels specific darkness
gloaming precedes night
as dawn precedes light
oracles sage
who follow the inventions
of natural law
specious claims to knowledge
from spurious fools
not knowing what they spew
acidic venom and fire
good intentions not manifest
help pave the road to Hell
the Ancient of Days
illuminates the way
to harmony and union

in Him and His creation.
Peace on Earth
goodwill toward all mankind!

If the World Goes Dark Tomorrow

para mis hijos, my children:

The world, our world, this world is presently as complex and unknown—to be so well known—as at any time in the recorded history of mankind.

It's easy in America and other first-world nations, where we are blessed with a multitude of modern amenities not found elsewhere in less industrialized countries, to be jingoistic, self-absorbed and downright cocky regarding our importance in the grand scheme of earthly existence. However, in reinforcing the above, I do fervently believe that as goes America, so goes the world!

I believe our survival and reliance on timeless values paradoxically balanced by individualism and community is why we lead the way, not because we have more value than the next faction of folks; but, precisely because the founding of our nation, though still containing flaws, was predicated on Judeo-Christian values and precepts inherent in natural law, common sense, goodness and a worldview amazed at the order visibly observed in the universe.

I quickly penned the following poem for my children; they are the "you" here. But, you are the you too! I want them to know if our hyper-communicative dependence on 21st-Century technology goes dark that I will see them if it is God's will, and if not, I will see them in the next world, because I believe...

If the world goes dark tomorrow
Know you are my prayer
Seek and ye shall find me
Cloaked in my Delta lair.

Guns, bullets and Bibles
My quartermaster's pay
The Almighty's provenance
Manna for today.

If I never see you
'Til Glory reigns supreme
My lil talks with God
Weigh more than they might seem.

If we're to be together
The Spirit will make a way
My eyes to the horizon
Until the Trumpets play.

My losses have been many
My victories have been few
Yet my greatest blessing
The Trinity, Madge and you.

If the world goes dark tomorrow
'Tis the Dark lord's plan
Trust that it's been sifted
Through God's omniscient hands.

Though the skies be crimsoned
Fear not the Foul one's fright
Look fervently to the heavens
Where abides Empyrean Light.

A Bright Star will guide us
If we are meant to see
Each other this side of Glory
If not.........Eternity!

∽

I Yearn for the Heather Hills

I yearn for the heather hills
Where history bleeds in sunlight
Though I've never been
I dream into the night

Reading the Scots of Old
Weathered, scarred and bold
Highland chiefs, proud and brave
Too soon, a pauper's grave

Hated when famine roared
Depopulating craig and spey
To America they came
To cities, big and grey

Though, I'm glad they came
America was all the more fitter
Yet, the island hills and shores
Lost a lot of stolid glitter

∽

Cemeteries at night

Cemeteries at night
Not my delight
Do dead stay dead
Not in my head

Lights in the gloom
Gloom in the night
Dead and the quick
Present and sick

Quick and the dead
Dance in my head
Peripheral vision
Distended with dread

Why am I here
What shall I see
Visions ephemeral
Costly yet free

Eyes in the dark
Dark are the orbs
Wary yet shiny
Hiding their lies

Tombs set askance
Fractures beneath
Etchings telling
Of last bequeaths

I shouldn't be here
Not in the night
Best I return
Long after light.

The dead by day
Hold not the same sway
The dead by night
A different sight.

Seek the Light.

Peace Will Calm the Waters

Awakened at three
Groaning at me
Waves lapping the tenuous shoreline
Startled by sound
Scary and bound
By nothing shackled or tethered
Long the leaf that flies at night
The wind not his brother's keeper
Whistlin' wind 'tis not the friend
Of him who lives beneath deciduous fragile
Limbs may bend
Squalling 'gainst the wind
As twigs and husks do prattle
Whistles and worries

Blusters and flurries
The Unseen makes Himself seen
Amid tremulous concern
Night worries burn
Fearing arbors so fragile
May God protect
The craning neck
Of eyes peeping with fright
Morning bids dark adieu
Thankful the tempest has ended
New day is fraught with unknowns not sought
What of the uncertain
The only Certain
Rent the curtain
Revealing the inner sanctum
Available to all
Earnest the call
To bend and be forgiven
The wind doth carry
And dare not tarry
Unto hinterlands wanting
Where still unseen
Harvester's glean
Waiting for fruit to ripen
Yes, 'tis the wind
A furious friend
Who carries missives cogent
Yet not opaque
Clear the lake
Undisturbed by motion
The storm may brew
A feverish stew
But Peace will calm the waters.

My Dog Dandy

by Little Billy Howell, still a sometimes little boy

I like my dog Dandy. He is a sweet little boy. He's smart. He's cute. He's funny. He has one crooked toof. He doesn't shed. He doesn't smell. He licks himself all clean like a cat.

He's soft and furry and likes to play and sleep and hump his pillow and big stuffed sheep. It seems to make him real happy.

He likes all people and most dogs. He chases squirrels and chipmunks. He is really fast. He's the fastest dog in the trailer park.

His real name is Dandy Lion Howell. He looked like a dirty dandelion when he was born. Some people call him the Dirty D. I call him the Dude.

He really likes his human Mommy. He likes me too. Now. I used to whup his butt when we were both littler. He likes me better now. We are buddies.

The End.

Rollercoaster Ride

I never liked rollercoasters
Beasts beyond control
Up and down
'Round and 'round
Airless above the ground

Jolts and jilts swirls and tilts
Bang, rang, clang and dang
Metal on metal wheel on steel
Fear and laughter peals

One sec up, one sec down
From shriek to grin to frown
Nanoseconds evoking change
Stasis left unbound

I do love adventure
Hints of the unknown
Pilgrim's Progress reset
Sojourns short or long

Yes life is a rollercoaster
One I can't control
Yet ride it I must
'Til old, dead and cold

Once ticket purchased
Rail and seat are found
Expectations muster
Courage best be found

With a wee-hoo we rise
With a woo-hee we fall
'Tween Heaven and Earth
Obeying a siren's call

For those unaccustomed
To letting go the reins
Tension in the body
Leads to further pain

Those loose as a goose
Will gander all the more
Due to their chill aura
They'll be not quite as sore

Engineer's design
Route set in advance
Slowly up the hill
Skyward is our glance

Just at the apex
When life is halfway through
We slowly start to realize
There's not much left to do

No more splashes to be made
White knuckling the safety bar
We plunge ever faster
Behind the first lead car

Hopefully bound for Glory
Faith our driving wheel
For those who avoided
Ole Dr. Faust's deal

The end approaches quickly
Often slow, then fast
We coast into the station
Our ride ended at last...

Not much left to do
Say, speak or pray
'Cept that our ride
Pleased Him on Judgment Day.

Lord please help me ride right…

What Threat Does a Hognose Pose

What Threat Does a Hognose Pose
A hognose poses no threat
He blusters and bows
He wiggles and throws
He huffs and puffs
And acts all tough
He flairs his head
Creating dread
Upended on his back
Acting like he's dead
Drama noodle is he

Cute as he can be
Fall not for his ruse
Just let his sweet self be
He ain' venomous.

Who Is Rich Folks

Who is rich folks
Is dey folks with lots and lots of money
Hab dey walls 'round milk and honey
Or do dey just gots more'n me

Rich folks is a wonder
For dey will tear asunder
All I have and hope to get
Just to get more an' a bit

Wealth measured 'gainst a crooked stick
Sho will never stick
'Cause dey's always someone colder
And always someone bolder
And always someone thinkin'
What is mines is his.

Da Good Book says not to covet
Dat which ain' none of mines
Dat book sho knows what's up
'Tween dem truthful lines.

Lord, help me to be thankful...
and not to want no mores
Than I'm s'posed to have
Please shut dem too-wide doors!

What I gots is good
And what is good I gots
So why oh Lord do I be thinkin'
I need lots and lots and lots…

Daily bread is daily
Bread is wheat and yeast
But I seems to think
E'ry meal need be a feast

If wealth be measured in grams
Like sugar in a sack
Dem scales would attest
Dat I ain' got no lack

My God He sits way high
But looks down mighty low
He knows what I be needin'
Fo' I even go to da sto'e

And His sto'e house nev'r empty
Full of alls I need
Yet my desire for more
Be's ev'dence of my greed

So if rich folks is just peoples
Who gots more than me
Then I'm surely rich folks
To dem with less than me!

Lord, help me…

I Saw Your Gaze Today

Penned upon seeing my despondency in another:

I saw your gaze today, though not directed my way; I feel your pain as few can. You are me, I am you.

Could I take your angst away, I would give you all I have, but what I timidly possess is intangible, yet very real...it is simply Hope...

Hope in the anomalous goodness of the Creator and sustainer of Heaven, Earth, and all things seen and unseen!

He's heard my cry—again and again—and cry again I will. He always answers, I rarely listen.

His assurance just a whisper, or his response found in the kindness of a stranger, perchance a nod or smile conveying promise; and at times, He speaks boldly through the wind or from a burning bush.

I hurt for you, yet not like you; your pain is unique because you are unique, your circumstances solely yours.

Pain shared is pain diminished; yet I flinch, afraid of my own ineptness and vulnerability. I'm so sorry!

I know God will help; I know He wants me to help; He commands it, yet I need help to help...

I am your glance, you are my mirror—what I behold frightens me. I fear our darkness; I recoil from our anguish; I am smothered by our despondency.

Am I the pharisee, the scribe or the Samaritan? Will I wish you well, and forget the tale of a pilgrim sorely in need?

Will I speak of the Eternal, neglecting the temporal, and feel as though I've shared?

Will a few bucks serve as salve for a deeply wounded soul, my pittance
    solving little—needs not met, nor guilt assuaged.

Am I my brother's keeper, or do I walk alone as he is alone, paths parallel
    to nowhere?

To share your load, I must be bold, and part with what I cannot keep:
    Faith, Hope and Love; the greatest of these is Love!

Only Guilty Man

Only Guilty Man
Here I stand
Only guilty man
Sequestered in a prison
Not of bars
Caged by scars
Graven by my undoing
Slashed and railed
Beyond the pale
Tethered by obsidian madness
Liberty a thought, a cry, a prayer
Submerged in the convict's lair

Hope purloined never enjoined
Sifted as chaff 'neath the scythe
Dank rot is rife
With pointless strife
Cannibals all are we
Hopefulness stained
Crimson with pain
Tormented by my subversion
Rocks cried out
With a shout
A plea for redemption
Time I must do
Until I'm through
Navigating cimmerian caverns
If I but will
Gaze to the hills
Where sunlight ne'er occludes
And 'umble myself
'Neath His mighty hand
Wed to a pardoned band
Of those redeemed, forgiven
Scars be healed
For the Kingdom's weal
Liberty reclaimed
Only God…

Ides of May

What a day
Docked sans a bang
Easin' in
'Neath the chin
Six feet from the virus
March blew hot
Rife with rot
Genesis East of West

Held near the vest
Kept from the West
Economies now in shambles
Opportunists led
With masks of dread
Intending to stifle
Both breath and rot
A polyglot
Hoping to dismantle
The brave and free
Who'd never be
Counted as elite
Middle class
Now out of gas
Backbone of a nation
'Tween plenty and none
This class doth run
Hither, dither and yonder
Yet when we run
Toward the Son
All will be well
Government matters
Yet now in tatters
Earth, its home confined
The Son of God
Cannot be prod
His shoulders broad and stout
Creation sings
The praise of kings
Seeking righteous order
'Tis no joke
For godly folk
To trust the seen Unseen
Despite our tough
We aren't enough
Fragile to the core
We pimp and preen
To be seen

As more than we're able
Head to toe
God doth know
We need Him more than ever
Acknowledgement of
Our need for Love
Is where new life begins…
We must break bread
To avoid the dread
Of impish isolation.

~

Cowered by the Lying Tongue

Cowered by the lying tongue
Nabobs run amok
Spewing incendiary phlegm
Couched in the specious
Thinking I am alone.

Alone not we
Gentler combatants
Cowered by evil intent
Fearing our hearts become the same
Kick against the goads we must
To stay alive and free

Towering titans above us
Yet far below
Lusting after that
Their own hands have avoided
In pursuit of our very souls

The wares they sell
Do cast a spell
Upon the naive pilgrim
Seeking solace from a crusted sphere
Void of redemption

Look not into the cerise eye
Intent on the devour
Look up to One
With Mercy's hands
Alone He can empower

Truth does triumph
Seemingly often late
Yet, Truth the final arbiter
Dismembers the lying tongue
Full of mischievousness and hate.

~

I Thought I Had More Time

Words echoing across a void.
No one knows the time
Hampster on a wheel
Moving yet stuck
Wanting the wheel's release
Not able to stop
Wishing for different
Assuming time will solve
What confounds the present
Time heals all
Not necessarily
Time affords opportunity
Too often squandered
Believing time will rectify
All that troubles me in the now
I thought I had more time
Now I sit alone
Missing my old friend
The laugher shared
Dinners set for two
Smiles and nods and warmth
Synapses unseen yet real
Connecting one to another
I thought we had more time
To fix our minor rubs
Seen only in our addictions
Times when anesthesia
Provoked more than it numbed
I thought we had more time
My heart now barren
Beating all alone
Dysrhythmia my constant tone
Warning others to steer clear
This man time left alone
Can God redeem the day
Yes, He can and will

But time marches on
My deeds leave me alone
With only His balm
To salve my claret scars
God can make me right
Rectifying wrongs
But deeds done in the night
Live longer than my wrongs
The light may draw the moth
Singeing my velvet wings
A chance I have to take
To flee the darkest night.
God help me!

Tank Man

Tank Man is the name ascribed to the unidentified Chinese man who stood blocking the departure of tanks from Tiananmen Square on June 5, 1989. The photo was taken by Jeff Widener of the Associated Press. What happened to this brave soul is unknown; however, he captured the hearts of freedom-loving souls around the world.

Ode to The Tank Man
Long may you stand
Against the ungodly statist demands

For those seeking refuge
Freedom & Truth
From governments caring
Too little for you.

Little you were
Large you'll remain
A beacon to many
A world gone insane.

To give one's life
Sweltering in strife
Never seein'
The freedom you're giving

Time and place
An unknown face
Fissures in stone
Standing alone

Many bestowed
What you are owed
You'll never see
Your final decree

Memories do fade
Sacrifices made
Heroism forgotten
In a world gone rotten

May tradition and pen
Count you a friend
Deeds treasured long
After you're gone

Ode to The Tank Man
Long may you stand
Against the ungodly, statist demands.

How Burned the Hands

How burned the hands
That slapped the Man
The Man from Galilee

Pharisee surge
The Roman purge
Ending a righteous life

Could they have known
What He had sown
This Man from Galilee

Slap God's own face
In time and place
What thought they to achieve

That they might know
Who took the blow
The Holy One Himself

Endured the shame
In His own name
The name God had bestowed

The skies grew dark
The devil's park
'Twas only 3:00 pm

The heavens roared
And demons scored
Thinking that they had won

But God knew best
And here's the rest
Here died the Son of God

Three days, the whale
Defined the pale
Where Jesus Christ was sent

The curtain rent
And Heaven sent
Its angels to adore

He stayed not dead
After he bled
Propitious was his deed

'Twas God's own Son
The Holy One
Eternity restored

He rose again
Negating sin
For those who lean on Him

Forgave the hand
That burned the man
Who didn't understand

He'd slapped the Man
Who took a stand
The Man from Galilee

Thank you, Lord! I believe!

Remorse

I lost a slight skirmish today
Though I didn't take a drink
Overstimulations
Brought me to the brink

Booze just a forethought
Not really in the plan
Yet, devouring specious pabulum
Got way out of hand

The guilt from acquiescence
And not doing as I ought
Led to more transgressions
Procuring less than nought

Racked with shame and guilt
I fed the Furies' fire
Temperance be damned
Genuflections to desire

Now, I'm feeling loathsome
Mephitic to the core
God, please help this addict
Shut Pandora's door.

Mañana is a new day
Release this yoke I must
Before these said addictions
Torment me with disgust.

It Shouldn't Hurt

It shouldn't hurt
to be a child,
nor one on the margins

where the mean prey,
and seek to slay
others not as strong

Darwin not wrong,
'tis the strong
who triumph over weakness

yet in the end,
the meek do win
as God's Eternal promise

the interim
is not the sum
of all we were and are

divorce, remorse
do run their course:
a tattered field of dreams

to prod the weak
and bloody the cheek
is a sign of weakness

resentments grow
while hatred flows
toward the defenseless

this world needs God
and not the rod
wielded by a despot

God, please come?
God did come;
yet, we killed Him too

He stayed not dead
He is the bread
for broken souls like Him/you/me.

Where Is Annabelle

Billowing waves on wind-swept waters
carry me away, to
distant lands,
where
mirages of the mind
tease my thoughts with shimmering,
simmering never reached oases
where real and surreal tango,
beckoning pilgrims like me
to come and see, feel and be,

something other than what is
and was, but what could be,
would be, should be,
if willing were we to flee,
and see what we could see,
perhaps a glint of Miss Annabelle Lee,
in her kingdom by the sea.

Victimization

Victimization
A foul impish tool
Ensnaring the simple
Beckoning the fool

Though roughshod be run
Yoke the oppressed
Chains emboldened
Heart fitful at rest

Darkness seeks it prey
Drafting those alone
Picking the weary
Stalking unknowns

Ensnaring outliers
Feeling alone
False sense of better
Chew not the bone.

Bone of contention
Needs no convention
Easily chewed
Prideful and shrewd

Cellophane Blues

While in detox in a treatment center prior to being transferred to JourneyPure in Eastern TN, I was struggling one night with a roommate's habit. Easily overstimulated and often affected by every bell, whistle, and noise not controlled by my dysfunctional self, I was about to snap in the middle of the night, but God and silently quoting the 23rd Psalm facilitated my not acting ugly, and I ended up really digging my roommate! A life lesson was learned, and anybody who knows me well knows the wrinkling of plastic can drive me insane!

Wakin' up at 3:00, what's wrong with me
Cellophane blues
Locked up in Rehab, not feelin' too far
Cellophane blues
Roomie ain' sleepin', sho gots me peepin'
Cellophane blues
Midnight rendezvous, snacks have got me blue
Cellophane blues
Plastic crinklin' loud, belchin' like he's proud
Cellophane blues
'Bout to lose my mind, better to be kind
Cellophane blues
23d Psalm, helpin' keep me calm
Cellophane blues
Earplugs and prayer, a desire to care
Cellophane blues
Out of Vistaril, maybe it's God's will
Cellophane Blues
Got dem Cellophane blues!

Casa De Macabre

Windows hazy
bad moon ascending
portends of malignancy lightly restrained
soon to be unfettered
evil hides not its lurking
inviting inquisitives in for a round…
Cacophonies of churlish laughter
felt more than heard
things older than man webbed in corners
restive yet motionless—frightened by more insidious evil
lurking beneath the pale
trawled by concupiscence—searching, always thirsty,
itching for innocence
shadows governed by edicts preceding man's dawn.

Welcome the immaculate
bid the pristine and the not-so enter…
come what may, fear is the mind's concoction, nothing to fear but itself.

What is fear but an unknown known, unknown in a knowing way
disquieted by predilections seen by unseens, fear of reprisals
unknown consequences for unseen behaviors known only by shadows.

Tread lightly, remember, the Fear of the Lord is the beginning of
    Wisdom.
Enter, but guard your heart...

∽

Balancing Man and Earth

Balancing man and Earth
Sadness and mirth
Stasis evades
Complexities pervade

Sense of well-being
Emboldened by Law
Sans Faith, Hope and Love
A certain lost cause

First-world parameters
Way too wide
Frog in the kettle
Acceptance in stride

Eminent domain
Governments adjure
Manifest Destiny
A specious cure

Respect is the answer
No easy task
Faith, Hope and Love
Will outlast the last!

∽

Look to the Heavens

Look to the Heavens
The Son yet still shines
He who winds the clocks
Ne'er runs out of time

The last tree standing
Is not so alone
Sap, bark and sinew
Are its flesh and bone

Thankful for roots
Light, water and soil
I reckon it's here
'Til God sheds its coil

Were I the last tree standing
Silence my refrain
Weathered and tattered
Exhausted from pain

Would I hold on to Hope
Knowing Him well
Anxiously awaiting
Donne's final bell?

Lord, I hope so!

Where Have All the Children Gone

Where have all the children gone
Forgotten, forfeit in time
Selective memory darkens
An already lurid crime

It began with Moses
Followed by Rachel's seed
Pharaoh and then Herod
Commenced the evil deeds

To kill God's Creation
Lucifer's great desire
Only God can save us
From hell's infernal fire

Innocence is manna
For God and devil twain
One desires to bless them
The other to kill and maim

Our children disappear
Yet we turn both blind eyes
Fearful the shadows may
Entangle us in lies

Horror, rank to chew on
Safer to think it not
But not safer for them
Drowning in Hades rot

What are we, what can we do
Enjoy our food and drink
While Jesus's lil ones
Are trafficked while we wink

Truly, the most precious
Of all a mom's travail
Is no longer secure
'Tis mankind's greatest fail

Oh Lord, please help us know
How to stand in the gap
Oh heart, be not quiet
We must stop this foul crap.

Kayaking on Moon Lake

On waters calm
Lands a pelican so light
Hunting fish below

The seagull flitters
As a kite without a tail
Seeing what's below

With eyes sharp as pikes
Airmanship never faileth
Guided by the light

Hastened swoops and drops
Upon the carpet beneath
Silently unseen

My kayak pierces
Amidst wind-churned waves so white
Lumbering to shore

The surface glitters
Sparkling diamonds on velvet
As die cast on felt

Molten crest bubble
'Neath a firmament so fair
Reflections shimmer

Horizon darkens
As sun settles 'neath the trees
Waves conclude blandly

Heralding the night
As day genuflects its lamp
Twilight bids the gloam

Earth begins its sleep
As waters concede their strife
Giving rise the night

When nocturnals prowl
Eyes dilated with desire
Seeking what they seek

Victuals for their young
Or asylum from despair
Tender is the dark

Edging toward the coast
My day yields unto the night
My skiff now ashore

The Moon is a love
Far beyond my just deserts
Thankfully, I sleep.

Salt Is Not the Devil

Salt is not the devil
Nor a blessing in excess
Guns are not the enemy
Best used when in distress

Salt is good for seasoning
And preservation too
If salt loses its nature
There's nothing to renew

Spirits are not a bad thing
If nipped with lots of care
But, for those in addiction
Buyer take note, beware

Most all matter is fruitful
Administered with care
But too much of most anything
Leads to great despair

The only thing in surplus
Not loved by every herd
Is that which is Eternal
God's goodness and His Word.

Mystery of Faith

Conceptually taken for granted
Rarely do we accede
The hidden things of God
Truths beyond our need

Does knowing lead to Faith
Does Faith lead to knowing
To know that is the Mystery
Still a mystery, yet unknown

If God be infinite, and He is
Because He says He is, He Is
He always was, the great I Am
Yet, came to us in form of man

Mary, mother, created by her own child,
chew on that more than a while
Mystery to Mystery, faith to Faith
Knowledge of the Mystery, still requires faith

Mysteries in the void
Treasures in the gloom
Truth must be pursued
Faith need be subsumed.

~

House 'Tween the Hedges

House 'tween the hedges
Patinaed, nondescript
Sodden porch bending
'Neath wind, rain, and deceit.

Loneliness exudes
Dampness beyond the pale
Furrowed rivulets of ash, grime,
pain and shale.

Fractious renderings of once
Stable unknowns
Glinting in the rare, shed rays
Of light's last glow.

Ghosts never quite peeped
Specters felt not gandered
Attic teeming with queries
Footprints long gone.

Floral prints decayed
Sullied by moth and time
Desiccated and blanched
Splendor in decline.

I know not your story
Blight the only tell
Ruin and occlusion
Bid adieu, farewell.

Yolanda's Shriek

The following was in response to a 14-minute sermon by Don Smith, rector at Grace Episcopal Church in Monroe, LA.

Don had been a young chaplain in his early ministry days at a hospital visiting seriously ill children. One child was gravely ill, likely not much time left in this life, but she never complained, was joyful always and her mother asked Don to baptize her!

A little new and unsure, he complied, and when she was baptized with items at hand in her hospital room, she shrieked with joy, causing raucous, Spirit-filled laughter and joy among her, her Mom, attending nurses and Don!

His retelling had me lifting my hands in praise and the following poem, a poor substitute for the event, was written as my response to joy not easily explained or understood:

> Yolanda's shriek was joy
> Not because of pain
> Though pain was ever present
> Joy entrenched in the Main
>
> The Main was not a man
> At least not as we think
> The Main always was
> Love's mysterious Link
>
> The Link to all that is
> Was, or will ever be
> Fathomless Creator
> Yolanda yearned to see
>
> Sick child was but four years
> Not much time was left
> Joy not capricious
> Spirit not bereft

Spirit forward-seeking
Complaints had she none
Willing to presume
Promises from the Son

Sacrament requested
Mother did beseech
Hospice chaplain willing
Not beyond his reach

A reach maybe stretching
Yet willing to comply
Baptize one so earnest
Apple of God's eye

Box filled with water
Shell used to ladle
Living water washing
Cleansing, soothing, able

Able to evoke
Shrieks of joy not pain
Pilgrim in God's Presence
Nothing left to gain

Lord, help me not be trifling
Frivolous or coy
May Yolanda's last shriek
Convert my tears to joy.

Drugs

Good boys and girls
Gone too soon
Reason defied
Glass hearts shattered
Societal edges jagged
Razors honed
Rusty blades tinged
Cuts divide
Slices sever
Hearts mended...
NEVER!

Petulant Peter

Petulant Peter
Has no meter
When measuring disrelish

To fuss and fume
Opaque the room
Painted by his displeasure

WRESTLING WITH WISDOM AT THE CROSSROADS

Against it all
Always his call
To those who heed his bromides

Nothing to say
Truthful or gay
Mercurial his temper

Goodness withstands
His squalid hands
Emboldened by the Holy

A taint on all
Who do befall
His last iambic measure

Carouse he might
Until the Light
Doth shed and shroud his nether

Avoid we must
His fatal gust
Of vice, varnish and venom

Return once more
To times of yore
Or we will all be tarnished

Seek good and right
With all our might
Or we'll be surely thwarted.

Yes, Peter must
In his disgust
Be shown a different highway

I Hold the Foul Thing Dearer

I hold the foul thing dearer
Nothing could be queerer
Than holding the thing nearer
Holding it much nearer
Than my wife
I loathe the foul object
Controlling every move
Yet, I reach for it's comfort
Thinking it will soothe
Whatever holes I have
Burned deep within my heart
Holes I am filling
With squalor a la carte
A smart phone it is thought
An addict's greatest treasure
Always handy, willing, and
Fraught with specious pleasure
The devil's in the details
Bytes, ones, zeros
Stirring up the masses
Turning friends to foes
The last times include
An increase in knowledge
How is this possible
A portal through Pandora's door
Distractions from what matters
Leaving souls in tatters
Eyes rarely meet
Concentration quite a feat
Moribund our fare
Empathy not a care
Yet the blue light draws us like a moth unto the flame
Delayed gratification
A thing of the near past
Truth now irrelevant
Just get us info fast

I fear we are no better
Yes, I would say much worse
For this ubiquitous invention
Belies the devil's curse
Turn it off.

She Called Me Daddy

The grandest words, ever heard, by any man alive; an utterance known, securing home, hearth and heart alike.

She called me Daddy, with the (y), why I'll never know; I was a fool, a broken stool, with legs wide splayed and flayed.

Thought I knew best, on my quest, to take care of my own; the own was me, sadly not thee, child whom I so adore.

Broken I'd been, my own worst friend, my children left alone; I spewed and cried, often lied, to me and to them.

'Twas not enough, left in a huff, faulting all but me; I could see, none but me, in my own reflection.

My pain was hard, leaving me scarred, unable to redress; what had come unseen, considered mean, snatching my seed away.

Could I have piped, with flute or fife, I would have led them away; but lips were cracked, heart attacked, full of venom's wrath.

If "rather be wronged," had been my song, I would have put them first; but jaded and jilted, my axis tilted, I clung to me alone.

But God restored, what was abhorred, mending much that was; one called me Daddy, and now I'm ready, to love and be forgiven.

Her love secured, has me assured, that God is on His throne; her forgiveness means, all the unseens, of Grace are freely given.

Thank you my love, for Agape love, undeserved by me; the cornerstone of our dear home, and all that love infuses.

She called me Daddy, now I'm ready, to let God help me be one!

She called me Daddy...

∼

Green Is All Around Me

Green is all around me
Verdancy secure
Spirit calming color
Living world's allure

Lushy leaves a blooming
Flowers add a spark
Green's soothing backdrop
Grotto for the lark

'Tis this lively color
That makes my spirit swell
Dwarfing trepidations
Fear and needs be quelled

How I wish that mammon
Had a different stain
Something that is needful
Causes so much pain

Money can destroy
What God has wrought in green
The world needs some balance
'Tween nature and machine

'Tis ocean's warm complexion
Slapping 'gainst the shore
God's promised redline
Earth flooded no more...

Green fades to brown
And other colors sure
But spring brings a rebound
Earth again verdure

Green, my favorite color.

CHILLY BILLY HOWELL

The Things We Lose

The things we lose, when we choose booze before the needs of others.

Insidious is, the spurious fizz that beckons to our throat.

Quench the dry, a little rye, will make us feel alright.

'Tis a lie, say goodbye, to all we thought we treasured.

A robber known, his wake windblown, a dustbowl is his measure.

Let not our eye, believe the lie, that alcohol's for all.

Some can drink, while others sink, far 'neath the surface foam.

And if I, believe the lie, which whispers you can do it.

Then I will end, 'round the bend, where sun has set in darkness.

What we lose, when we choose, amber's grave reflection.

For us it seems, as it gleams, we are strong as others.

Yet others can, still the hand, while mine twitches unceasing.

I best avoid, the stygian void, where I have walked the line.

To dance once more, near Gehenna's door, would seem to be quite foolish.

I fear next time, would be the time, when ticks my clock no more.

The things we lose, when we choose booze, before the needs of others.

Dandy and Daddy

Dandy and Daddy lyin' in bed.

One rolled over to the other and said, "Hey Big Boy, whatcha wanna do?

Lie right here, how 'bout you?"

"Works for me," the lazier one said, never even blinking, nor moving his head!

Neither worth killin', lazy as can be, lazybones lyin' 'neath the big shade tree!

Scratchin' our bellies, liftin' our legs, we too lazy even to beg.

Life is rough, tough as can be, dat's why we lyin' under dis hea tree.

Doin' all this thinkin', wears us out, but we doin' the right thing, ain' no doubt.

Some say we triflin', some say we sorry, shiftless even works, we ain' got no worries.

Lyin' in the shade, we got it made, me and Dandy…lyin' 'neath the puuucan tree…

We free!

Earl and Ginger, What a Pair

Earl and Ginger, what a pair,
Melding, meshing, sans a care
Roiling in candor, rancorous not,
Bless this affable, mellifluous lot
Spicy by nature, zesty yet pale,

Ginger belying a pretense of frail
Earl Grey, bold, Bergamot to core,
Earthy yet elegant, steeping in lore
Together refreshing, settling their lees,
Arguably two of my favorite teas.

Never a Civil Word

Never a civil word is heard amongst the drama-ridden
Sunup, sundown, never found edifying mentions.

Lambast and curse, fear the worst, provocateur's caprice
Start a fight, end the night rife with wrath's delight.

Roll the dice, never nice, craps always a given
Hide and fret, lose the bet, today will not be different.

Hearth and home feel alone amongst foul tongues a waggin'
Peace unknown in the home where tempers flare in clusters.

You meek beware the fowler's snare always baited waiting
Sticks and stones may break some bones, yet words are just as harmful.

Seek His grace in a place where only He can enter
If hearts be sound, God's playground 'tis where safety resides.

God can fill a bitter pill to brim and overflowing
With Love and Grace in any place where His presence is wanted. Peace.

I Lost Another Friend Today

I lost another friend today
Sadly, in the same old way
Too many lost to nectar divine
'Tis sad what it leaves behind

It's wake is wavy
A perilous froth
None untarnished
Flame to moth

The siren's call
Draws us in
Wrecks our lives
Begins again

Seeking souls
Promises made
Empty contracts
Never paid

I know its pain
Aware of its draft
Yet still am drawn
To evil's craft

He is a liar
As is his juice
Take a sip
Hyenas loosed

Not all are bitten
Not all succumb
But many of us
Under its thumb

We must resist
Cease and desist
My brother's gone
He will be missed!

All honor to your name! Much love and Peace, SPG!
In hoc,
Chilly

The Soul of an Addict

The Soul of an addict
Such a tender thing
'Tis no grand wonder
Life's such a nasty sting.

We yearn for peace
Acceptance too
We seek relief
In the devil's brew.

Our souls are tender
Our sensibilities frayed
Walking live tightropes
Night into day.

∼

My Heart a Seismic Seam

My heart a seismic seam
Waiting to explode
My brain a fault-lined fissure
Expecting to implode
Truth the only anchor
Capable to hold
Cavernous substructures
Predisposed to fold
Nano-second thoughts
Kaleidoscopin' brightly
Not-tethered to goodness
Paint palettes unsightly
Human mind and body
Complex in full detail
2nd Law Thermal dynamics
Ensures entropy's fail
As carbon-based entities

Recede toward their demise
The only Hope for mankind
We must lift our eyes
Gazing unto the Heavens
Where Majesty rules the skies
From dust to dust
As iron doth rust
Our bodies disappoint
Yet spirit and soul
Never fold
For Judah's Lion is bold!

Seek Him while we may...

Hegemony Foul

Best not poke the Russian Bear.
Let the Afghan nomad roam.
Bend not the knees of the Vietnamese.
Colonialism's reach will cause a breach.
Largesse hard to maintain.

Rome tried, Bonaparte denied.
Alexander's demise began the rise of the Hellenic age.
Ending with Rome collapsing the dome of Macedonia's rule.

Egypt's slain would be the bane of those enslaving others.
Cycles repeat, mankind replete with desire to control others.

Hegemony rules when utter fools care not for other's fate.
Sparta ruled until the gruel of Persian defiance.

Peace ensues when might subdues without a blade engaged.
Both be strong, let not the wrong, fester into fury.

The Prince of Peace came not to lease the strongman's able warriors.
He came, he gave, a newer wave, of how to love another.
No able arms, no magic charms, His blood was sufficient.

Wide Awake on Prednisone

Wide awake on prednisone
Wrote a poem in the zone

Waters haunt
Yet they draw
Source of life
In the thaw

Deep to deep
Spring to fall
Ebb and flow
Master's call

Heat gives rise
To wind and wave
Nature's obeisance
Defies the rave

God subdues
The torrent's rage
His commands
Still the gage

His decree
Seas must cease
Rainbow declares
Creation's lease

Fire consumes
Mountains crumble
Water desecrates
Yet just a rumble

Water woos
Haunts me still
Moth to flame
Hook to gill

He Is, I Am
God bespoke
Wide awake
Yet not woke.

A Pleasant Wilderness

A pleasant wilderness is...

...a safe haven bearable with Hope in the placement of the Almighty

...a season of unentangled instruction void of worldly incitements, bereft of unventilated overstimulation

...a background steeped in golden splendor, suffused with unapproachable Light, and uncomplicated by cares laboring beyond subsistence

...a land where the sparrow is watched, the raven never goes hungry, manna is daily, and the breathe of the Creator—the Ancient of Days, the Great I Am, the Always Was, the Always Will be the Evermore—nourishes every follicle of the spawned

...a time and space in place—broad, undefined and reflective—never measured linearly nor constrained by knowns

...a season beyond Vivaldi's Four, a parameterless kingdom where Paideia reigns supreme—God instructs, mankind listens; God coaches, mankind practices; God and man Socratically dialogue

...a duality reflecting Kingdom paradoxes painstakingly embraced by Job, Jonah and Jacob, none strangers to wrestling in the wilderness, where mano-a-mano and mano-a-Dios are membrane-less double entendres, best understood in the presence of the Host of Heaven's armies in a suzerainty not of our making nor command

...a time for everything beneath the Son

Lord, teach me now, in a wilderness of your construction, while my breathe remains, though my head and heart grow hoary and weary; strengthen the little that endures, and prepare your weak and fallen one for the battle not of my choosing and not fought by my strength! To you, and you alone, doth my allegiance bear...

CHILLY BILLY HOWELL

Sitting on the Square

Sitting on the square, sans a care, white noise methodically lapping 'gainst the sidewalk.

Herfin' stogies, eyes peeled for bogies, thoughts rockin' gently in a pirogue of my own illusion.

Sky fabled-blue, a corn-flowered hue, students hidden in towering dorms lightly studying, connected via ephemeral synapses to ivy-laden halls bathed in lonely ether.

Collegiate watering holes shuttered, "Covid-19" roundly uttered, in-person tutelage no longer a mandate, as pigskins deflate into autumn.

"What a Wonderful World," seldom now heard, Louie's grinnin' puffy-cheeked visage only a felicitous memory as nascent ones pine for spring, long 'fore winter has portended its chill.

The world in flux, a virus the crux, the unseen seen and likely embellished.

Maskin' the norm, preceding the storm, morning red's sky a sailor's dire warning.

'Tis not the plague, blame not The Hague, nor any seat of power; a lab might be ground zero.

Life: a soul-making vale, Keats did rail, life and death do instruct and ebb as the Moon-driven tide ripples ancient, endless shorelines.

"Already dead," screams in my head, "Look what you have lost!"

If already dead, I made my own bed, and lost more than I can imagine.

The Piper pied loud, lost in the crowd, taking the children with him.

How to go on, feeling alone, memories the curse of the fallen.

God has a plan, I'm just a man, one He has forgiven.

Forgiving myself, placing scars on a shelf, is where I fall short of center.

Life is a gift, must bridge the rift, if I'm to stay clean and sober, a liminal segue to the Eternal.

God help this man, show me the plan, to strengthen what little remains.

This old-broken soul, seeks to be whole, your Holiness is what I must chase! God help me?!

∼

The Cabal of Vile

The cabal of vile
Ranges for miles
Where children's innocent dreams devolve into nightmares never understood nor fathomed beyond those already dreamless propagating the same. SHAME!

Existing in the realm of the Supernatural is either good or evil, symbiosis melds not oil and water, benevolent entities are not sired by a union of good and evil. The supernatural always is found traversing the plains seeking to influence…

If sheer evil exists—it does—then imputations foul, sulphuric boils from the Father of Lies, casts asunder from Heaven for pride befitting a fool, will surely "seek to steal, kill and destroy" all that is good, pristine, innocent, guileless, and pleasing to the Father and the family.

Evil thrives when good dies and when "good men and women do nothing!"

Satan is insatiable!

Through Herod he slaughtered Rachel's gendered seed not exceeding their second year! He continues the yearly elimination of—now totaling over 50,000,000—children of Promise, fearfully and wonderfully made by the Great I Am, the Ancient of Days, the glorious, majestic Creator and Sustainer of all that is…

The sower of familial discord daily destroys the intended fabric of society sustainable—divorce, abuse, abandonment, strife, despondency, alienation…

The foul one roams the Earth, a ravenous fully-maned lion, deprived of his thought-to-be stately inheritance, seeking the wanton blanket destruction of all, the eradication of nascent hopefuls—created with and for purpose, slaughtered for none.

'Tis not enough to end the hopes of mankind before their introduction, he must thoroughly defile their stain-free existence with prurient acts committed by those sullied with puerile—tethered and obsessed with self-gratifying desires never to be slaked.

I speak of the children, robbed of hope, fondled grotesquely for the insatiable pleasure of the gropin' groomers, inspired by the fallen one, masquerading as an Angel of Light!

Godly people, everywhere, give not up the Good Fight, "go not gently into that good night!" Rage, rage, against the waning of Thomas's light!
God, please protect our children!

Acid Rain, Mammon's Stain

Acid rain, mammon's stain, killing all that's good.

Progress and abundant amenities too often reflect hearts no longer tender to empathy's continual cry pleading relief for the weary and dispossessed.

Money and things not inherently evil, yet value relegated is where begins the rub.

It's a short ride, so hide not your head in the sand, as the hourglass begins its fateful tilt.

What will our children's children say, if we seize not the day, as we too gently ease into that good night sans a fight for rectitude and right, flush with our own import and comforts, as resources intended for our descendants are squandered upon selfish compulsions, erotic sensibilities void of common sensical restraints presaged upon natural law, and wasted like crude oil in the ocean?

Money and progress are needful, but need to be checked—individually and corporately.

Seize the day, in a way, that pleases our Creator!

∼

Blood, Blood, and More Blood

Oceans couldn't contain
what flowed from my veins
veins sliced deeply
front to back.

I didn't want to do it
I just couldn't see through it
a forest thick with angst
and fraught with pain.

I have now one regret
I did not pray and fret
to struggle more and ask
my friends for help.

An isle unto myself
phone upon a shelf
I left it so I couldn't
cry out for help.

Now I am afraid
knowing I should pray
aware only a miracle
could save my fate.

I still resist a cry
having bought the lie
that life has no meaning
at its core.

Only now I get the wonder
of life on a frozen tundra
fed by a God of plenty
not of dearth.

Oh, that I am too late
ambling toward the gate
a gate of no return
but one of fate.

Fate implies no hope
yet hope I still yet may
if I could survive
just one more day.

My eyes now growing dim
I think that I see Him
holding out His hands
marred and scarred by holes.

His robe ablaze and white
illuminating night
the night of my folly
in the extreme.

Lord, I start to say
now I look full away
reckoning I no longer
have the right...

In silence He seems to say
my son, 'tis not the way
look up, rejoice, for
Salvation comes today.

"Oh Lord," I begin to pray,
"I've truly lost my way
would you reach out
and heal my scars and heart?"

"My child," He intones,
"They didn't break My bones
I shed My unstained blood
all on My own."

It is not too late
to choose the narrow gate
cry out while your breath
yet still remains.

Oh Lord, I've been a fool
life was more than cruel
but not so cruel I couldn't
have picked a better way.

Forgive me I implore
shut not the opaque door
the vanguard of those
who yearn for more.

I now see there's more
than settling every score
resentment keeps me
in an erstwhile fog.

Open wide my eyes
protect me from the lies
foul utterances loosed by
the Prince of Lees.

Fibs told on the cheap
stacking up a hilly heap
of lives littered and
devoid of hope.

Silence the foul one's voice
help me make the choice
a choice designed to
save my very soul.

I choose before I die
I beg, implore and cry
for mercies undeserved
please help me now...

My blood now running cold
wishing I had sold
all I had for one more chance
to stick around.

I begin to swoon
life ebbing way too soon
knowing I have lived
my life in vain.

I gander at my wrist
no strength to make a fist
blood shed in folly
haste and pain.

I no longer see
what's right in front of me
my eyes grow faintly dim
as does my heart…

…….silence…….

…awakened with a start
blood coursing through my heart
through veins no longer sliced but on the mend.

Life giving life to life
almost destroyed by my own strife
but now saved by Grace
blood conquered blood.

The Luddites Have it Right

The Luddites have it right
Technology a fright
Pen and paper will be fine.

The devil holds in sway
Those he's led astray
Selling progress as The Way.

Progress not the prob
The devil he doth rob
God of Glory due His name.

Skynyrd's Simple Man
Spells out the plan
For a youngster's happiness.

To the Unknown Waitress

To the unknown waitress
May your strength never fade
Your glory rooted in service
Yet treated like a maid.

Long hours on yo feets
Stressors back at home
Children needs attention
Daddy be long gone!

Serving mens for tips
Often slim at best
Hopin' for some kindness
Yet offered a sausage fest.

A wink, a nod, a grope
Plus an extra dollar
Ain' gonna entice
A tired waitress to holla.

Treat her with respect
And tip a few more bills
But that does not entitle you
To get up in her grill.

Folks gripin' 'bout a burger
Gripin' about dey tea
Acting like da King and Queen
Themselves only they see.

She smiles 'cause she cares
She smiles 'cause she can
That's the job of service
Now act like a gentle man.

Her kids at home is hungry
Her kids at home is sick
So men use yo head
Quit acting like a prick.

You surely ain' dat special
You sho ain' dat good lookin'
So leave the lady 'lone
And do yo own dang cookin'.

You'll spend ten extra dollars
On another dirty martini
So please stop wonderin'
If she's hankerin' fo' a weenie.

Take that ten dollars
Out of yo own hand
Leave it on the table
Be a grown-ass man.

Treat her like a sister
Treat her like a mother
Treat her like a Princess
Act like her big brother.

God bless her children
God bless her home
God bless all waitresses
Known and unknown.

Show some respect.

I Pose for Others

I pose for others, showing them what I will, not who I am, 'cause I don't know; I am who I am, but who am I?

I've spent my entire life either genuflecting or stiffening my neck, based on flawed perceptions, gears grinding with little purpose, tread smoldering on pavement, deeds left undone.

Search and rescue, search and destroy, search and adapt. Chameleons fascinate. Can they be trusted? Only as far as the color one sees.

I pose for safety; I pose for peace; I pose for the greatest and the least; most of all, I pose for Peace—Peace matters to a life in tatters; yet, the Prince of Peace needs posers the least!
Be who we are!

Winter Arrives

Pelicans in flight
Geese overhead
Sumac shades red
'Tis good for my head

Winter's barren approach
Fall's bequeth
Seasonal affectation
Need some relief

Walking outside
Stretching the soul
Balance and health
Ulterior goals

Mostly, I need
Grace and Godspeed
Love, Joy and Peace
Ultimate relief

Short on strength
Long on need
Daily bread
My best feed

Look to the sun
Hope it does shine
If not, the Son
Not hard to find

Hand-stitched Lacerations

Hand-stitched lacerations
from scar tissue reopened has sadly become the norm for combatants
 wounded by love, antipathy, or something in between.

Cauterized scars rarely heal completely, nor do they disappear in resent-
 ment's gorge; they merely mend, poorly—in time—'til memories
 serrate quondam's anguish buried deep 'neath mounds of melding
 spite, animus, newness, and hope.

Heal and tear, heal and tear, hard to bear alone; good friends matter, and
 the Lord of Hosts offers salve for garnet wounds quickened like fish
 gills silently pleading for air inside the batture on gritty shorelines.

We stitch and stitch in vain, bearing the pain of a past no longer existent,
 flogging ourselves afresh for deeds done and left undone, opening
 wounds not quite healed.

What to do?

With God's help…let go the past, cast not our eyes too far in the future,
 live in the present and sincerely desire and allow God to apply
 Gilead's balm! Only God…

Anthem of First-World Shame
Thoughts of Father's Day

"Cats in the Cradle, silver spoon, Little Boy Blue and the Man in the Moon!"

Harry Chapin understood,
busy is the bane of I wish I could.

Gotta make a splash, make that cash,
fam gonna blow away just like ash.

Divorce and abortion searing our souls,
gotta make sure we reach our goals.

Sun comes up, sun goes down,
most parents just can't be found.

Parents too busy, kids the same,
table time lost, name of the game.

God don't matter, He's the same,
we're too occupied playing our games.

Shabbat long gone, down time too,
sorry my Loves, gots no time for you.

Know I love you, dear to my heart,
sorry the horse is behind the cart.

I'm workin' hard, hard as I can,
want to provide like my Old Man.

You deserve the best my child,
just give me a little more while.

CHILLY BILLY HOWELL

We'll get together soon I say,
I need only one more day.

Yes, we'll get together then my child,
I just need a little while.

Say, my child, whatcha doin' today,
think you'll be heading your Pop's way?

Just too busy, I understand,
you're just like your old man.

Well my child, enjoy your time,
I wasted time chasing mine.

I miss you........................

Covid-19 Belly Blues

My belly is extended
Covid-19 gots me blue
Done 'bout ruint my bidness
What's a fella to do

Be thankful I ain' hongry
Be thankful I ain' too blue
My belly evidences
It grew and grew and grew

I blame it on the virus
Lack of discipline at its core
Regardless of the timing
I've a Disease of More

Fat is in my family
Fat is in my head
Fat is all around me
As I lie prone in bed

I sho got some blues
Covid be fo realz
I may not be drinkin'
But I ain' missed no meals

Just like dat ole camel
My hump and sto' house full
I wanders in the desert
Fat belly cruel with gruel

It makes it hard to sit
It makes it hard to stand
It makes it hard to get up
My belly it is grand

It shows I ain' malnourished
It means that I am well
It's proof that I be eatin'
When rings the dinner bell

I sho do wish it'd shrink
Even a tiny bit
But it just might sustain me
In case dat Covid hit

I hurt for those who sick
The whole world goin' blue
My belly is a growin'
What's a fat fella to do

Maybe cut my portions
Eat a little less
Get my fat-ass movin'
Dat plan sounds tha best

My belly it still growing
What am I to do
Try to get some balance
Until dis Covid through.

Lord, he'p me!

Hairline Fractures

Hairline fractures in the main
Destabilizing edifices at the core
Division divides all that is
Disseverance destroys unity
Puppet master unrestrained
Not often seen but felt
Destroying harmony and peace

Solidarity be damned
A divided anything cannot stand
God separates sheep and goats
He doesn't divide His people
The devil does, seeking to
Kill, steal and destroy
Peace on Earth and
Goodwill toward mankind
Resist him we must
Leaning on the Lord
And the Golden Rule
Do unto others as we would
Have then do unto us
We desire not division in our lives
So let's not divide other's lives
If it does take a village
Internecine warfare will destroy
The children of the raising
We don't have to agree
Iron will sharpen iron
But fellowship we must
From dust to dust to dust
Allied strands must band
Strengthening the whole
Which must in turn resist
The devil's vilest wiles
Hairline fractures we must mend
Upon this we need depend…
Lord, Help us!

Hate Has No Color

Hate has no color, hate has no shade, yet wide its shadow doth casts—
 portending intentions foul, separating friend and foe alike.

Do we hate because we were first hated; do we love because we first were
 loved?

A perennial question…

Answers found in one's relationship or lack thereof with the One who
 "brung" us—The Creator and host of Heaven and maintainer of
 Earth and all that is.

The Lord strong and mighty, who is Love and is the Great I Am!

We are the human condition, birthed in sin, yet imbued with a God-
 shaped vacuum
longing for the filling of a Spirit who is God Himself, who is Love,
and who wants us to love even the haters who know not Love!

Feet Marching High on Poplars

Summer breeze in the trees, feet marching high on poplars. God's answer to petitions comes in many unexpected forms.

David pled and God led, victorious scores of triumphs, reputation spread far o'er land and sea.

God will not stay mocked, nor respond half-cocked to earnest pleas for aid.

He says to ask and never bask in victories and methods used before—they are of the past.

The Creator's role, ne'er inveigles the soul to respond with casuistic intent.

We need just plead, in time of need, for God's favor in all things.

Patiently wait for the gate of understanding to open wide, revealing gilded treasures kept hidden for the day.

The Host of Heaven's Armies may answer in a whisper, a maelstrom of wind stirred, or in the sound of feet marching high atop the poplars.

Slowly settle, watch not the kettle, the boil will surely come.

Ask and see, the I Am is He; and He will answer...when and how He answers...Just abide and listen...for the sound of feet marching high on poplars.

The Days of Wine and Roses Nevermore

"The days of wine and roses laugh and run away like a child at play
  Through the meadow land toward a closing door
  A door marked "nevermore" that wasn't there before
  The lone-ly night discloses just a passing breeze filled with memories
  Of the golden smile that introduced me to
  The days of wine and roses and you."

— JOHNNY MERCER

The good life's momentary peaks rarely linger
Fondly treasured and thankfully remembered
Meteoric splashes
Temporal ripples
Disappearing coils of memory
Buried 'neath life's encroaching ugly
Life inhered in soused furrows
Chronic trench foot a constant companion
Essence mired in immutable vicissitudes of laboring paradox
Purposeful pilgrims trekking the unknown
Seeking solace from occluding portals of promise
Nevermore fissures linking past to present
Shuttering forever serene sentiments
Birthed in prelapsarian innocence
Nurtured briefly at leisure's bosom
Fattened with the milk of specious safety
Protected by fading veils of false security
Wine's uncorking a temporal solace for wounded souls
Now a constant mocker
For those too lean to metabolize
Roses resplendent
Nascent leaves of saturated velvet
Softening eyes into crinkling lines of pleasure
Ending desiccated and weary
Receding aromas bereft of consolation
Fluttering from verdant meadow to vales steeped in darkness
The Days of Wine and Roses an apparition

Once a golden smile
Now a testament to Nevermore...

My Sister is Submissive

My sister is submissive
And we know it's true,
Only 'cause she told us,
'Til her face was blue!

Her hubby is fortunate
Wow! Such a fine dame
She even rubs his back
Prior to every game!

Cooking is her specialty
Sweetness a hallmark
She even glows and glitters
In the pitch-black dark!

How I envy her hubby
Her wisdom in the fold
And she'll remain submissive
Long as he does as told...

Grumbling and Complaining

Grumbling and complaining
Long a human fault
Wanting more than needing
More always sought

Consumers never satisfied
Long game rarely heeded
Excess supersedes enough
Growth surely impeded

Thankful hearts struggle
Where cornucopia is chief
More we have, more we want
Surfeit sans relief

Hallmark of the human
Broadened at the core
Thankfulness our yen
Never keeping score

Consequences catch up
Eventually with the greedy
Daily bread enough
Even for the needy

Manna from Elysium
Never spoiled with leaven
Pure and rich with substance
All good things from Heaven!

Thank you God!

Shades Are What We Recognize

Shades are what we recognize
Shades are what we see
Shades are what distinguish
You from them and me

The biggest shade we have
Is deep within our soul
The heart is hard to see
Obsidian, red or gold

The outer person known
By shades, hues, veneer
Shallow misconceptions
Rife with subtle fear

Shades display contrast
Distinctions what we see
Yet shades are just one color
More similar, I feel, are we

Our visage may be known
Epidermis just skin deep
Yet, God sees the heart
Never slumbers, nor He sleeps

A soul with a body
Or a body with a soul
The inside matters more
Or so we have been told

We look on the outer
God looks on the inner
It's what on the inside
That marks us all a sinner

Yet, fallen are we all
Need cleansing every day
Yet destitute we're not
Jesus made a way.
His sacrifice propitious.

∼

Alipius Knew Better

Alipius knew better
His raising taught him so
The arena, never should he go
Bloodsport held no sway
The arena, not his Appian Way
However, on one sundry day
Friends cajoled he go their way
Alipius assumed his strength enough

Having eschewed the rougher stuff
Combatants blood, and fans roar
Opened his eyes, Pandora's door
Consumed by lust and taste for blood
He now wallowed in Satan's mud
Augustine notes, he later turned
Back to God and all he'd learned
The sad lesson in this old tale
Best avoid beyond the pale.

∼

Seen and Unseen

I never knew why, existed earth, water and sky. Yet, marvelously designed were they.

I always accepted, due to my upbringing, that God existed, that He was good and that He loved me and everybody…
particularly all the children of the world: red, yellow, black and white, and later learned, brown.

These were givens.

I am eternally thankful to my mother for her emphasis on Faith and my father for his emphasis on pragmatism. The two can coexist, but often don't.

The Stoics understood pragmatism and its emphasis on virtue and outcomes, the early Christians better understood Grace, redemption and forgiveness.

In the Apostle Paul's letter to the nascent, 1st century AD Roman church—which believed in Christ's divinity, life, death, and resurrection—he states that God's existence should be apparent in the seen world.

This should lead us to inquire into who created the marvelously designed "seens," then into the metaphysical, beyond-reason "unseens," where treasures exist beyond compare.

In the pantheon of pluralistic, nativistic religions, assumptions, isms and philosophies, many have missed Him, the Creator of Heaven and Earth, and have inerrantly worshipped His creation.

AFTERWORD

Madge and I hope this three-part book will be a catalyst for individual reflection and an incentive for small group discussions.

"Wrestling with Wisdom at the Crossroads," as a project and as a real-life, real-time endeavor, has been a journey filled with failure, self-inflicted pain, and Faith. This unusual representation of my walk through distress, addiction, recovery and a very real renewing of my faith in God, is my somewhat opus of discovery and re-discovery of what matters and what doesn't.

Though this book does not fit any distinct genre, I hope the aphorisms, poems, and particularly the devotional companion, will in some way bless, intrigue and spur the reader to self-discover the Wisdom God offers those who seek!

I humbly conclude that God is who He says He is, and He will do exactly what He says He will do.

Cheers! Chilly Billy, a.k.a. Malachi Montroy

ACKNOWLEDGMENTS

This book, all it contains, and my very life would not have been possible without my wife, Madge Marley Howell. She has always seen good in me, when there was very little; she has stuck by me in good times and plenty of tough times; and, most importantly, her simple, yet held-deeply Faith in God and His Word has inspired me to continue wrestling with God and His Wisdom at every late-life juncture.

My parents, Roundman and Mama Jane: for your parentage, safe upbringing full of comfortable amenities, and, most importantly, for your medley of erudite pragmatism and Faith. I was never easy to understand, yet you loved me still.

My maternal grandmother, Granny: categorically, the best combination of wisdom, meaningful education and plain old common sense I have ever witnessed.

My girls: for your love and forgiveness for my legion of mistakes as a damaged, limited father. Your love for me is a sustainable joy.

Corinne: your acceptance of me as a late-life step-dad and your solid, perceptive input into this book is immeasurable.

Carolyn Wiley, Rose & Pearl Publishing: what a providential Godsend when you agreed to co-labor on this project. Thank you!

Neil White: for advice on how to approach our idea for this book when it was in its nascent stage and for answering all of our questions.

Susan Trionfo and Sherye Green: for being a source of encouragement as published authors.

My Recovery group: for helping me live one day at a time. We do recover and the program works if we work it.

Michael Card, C.S. Lewis, G.K. Chesterton, Francis Schaeffer, and Chuck Colson: five men whose philosophy, theology, worldviews, and unique perspectives on Faith—and its relevance to history and present-day living—have demonstrably influenced my thinking through the clear times as well as the cloudy days.

ABOUT THE AUTHOR

Chilly Billy is a self-described Contrarian, Agrarian, Riparian, Prelapsarian docent of dubious Quixotic distinction, who still tilts at windmills. Having lived in many places and having worked in myriad occupations, he is thankful to have returned to the Mississippi Delta, where the flat lands, pace of life and felicitous folks all provide his sensitive self the Grace to live a redeemed life only God could provide after a lifetime of missteps, miscues, and poor path choices. Remo Ergo Sum: I paddle, therefore I am. He still wrestles!

ABOUT THE ARTIST

Madge let her art lie dormant for many decades before its return in recent years. Some works were created for this book, others in the years leading up to it. In painting and drawing she feels near to God, seeking not perfection but presence —trusting each stroke as an expression of surrender to His will. What she creates is not meant to be flawless, but faithful. Her prayer is that the drawings stir deeper reflection—on the aphorisms, poems, and devotional companion, and on the reader's own life and choices.

For past and future musings, visit: www.deltabohemian.com

ILLUSTRATION INDEX

BY MADGE MARLEY HOWELL

Battling Choices..220
Beckon..322
Crane on a Post...295
Delta Field Highway..222
Dog in Barren Field...314
Ducks on the Moon..288
Emory's Field..247
Eye to Eye Man...225
Faces Before Crosses...1
Geese Rising over field..308
Green Tree...293
Guntersville Paddle..234
Hurting Child...262
If the World Goes Dark...238
Kokopelli Tree..236
Little Tree Reflection...319
Lone Kayaker on the Moon..217
Macabre House...266
Man in Water..229
Man Walking Away 7
McMillin Tree #1...286
McMillin Tree #2...306

ILLUSTRATION INDEX

Montroy Cemetery..242
Moon Lake in the Cold Morning............................244
Morning Flight over Burkes....................................269
Ocean Man..255
Ochre Trees by water..281
Pecan Cows...283
Poles Reflected...303
Schoolbus Bird...297
Shadow Man Reflected..251
Shovel Man..278
Tank Man 257
The Cave..273
Theodore..310
Tree on Hill...275
Whistle on Levee...232

www.ingramcontent.com/pod-product-compliance
Lightning Source LLC
Chambersburg PA
CBHW060414010526
44107CB00006B/683